# HALLOWE'EN: TREAT OR TRICK?

# HALLOWE'EN:
## Treat or Trick?

**DAVID PORTER**

MONARCH
TUNBRIDGE WELLS

First published 1993

**British Library CIP Data**
A catalogue record for this book is
available from the British Library

ISBN 1 85424 237 7

Produced by Bookprint Creative Services
P.O. Box 827, BN23 6NX, England for
MONARCH PUBLICATIONS
P.O. Box 163, Tunbridge Wells, Kent TN3 0NZ
Typeset by J&L Composition Ltd, Filey, North Yorkshire
Printed in England by Clays Ltd, St Ives plc

# CONTENTS

# INTRODUCTION

This is a book about Hallowe'en. It's not a book about witchcraft, satanism or black magic. It's not a sociological work or a historical tract. It's not a theological argument (though it comes from a Christian perspective). It discusses all of these to a greater or lesser degree, and a wide range of other subjects, but only insofar as those subjects relate to Hallowe'en.

Some pamphlets, videos and other publications about Hallowe'en are really about witchcraft or some other related subject; but in this book I have simply attempted to gather together facts about the festival of Hallowe'en in the past and in modern times, and to put those facts into a variety of contexts. I have also drawn on my own work over the past few years in the fields of fantasy literature, fantasy games, the media, and children's play.

I have written in response to an increasing concern from parents, teachers, youth workers, church workers and many others. That concern reflects a sharp rise of publicity, both in the commercial world and in the media and entertainment industries, which has pushed the subject of Hallowe'en to the fore; each year, as October nears its end, the discussions begin all over again. I hope that this book will help people to make up their own minds about Hallowe'en, and to discuss the subject with others in a constructive way.

This book is less a piece of original research than a survey of information contained in a large number of other books. Many people have helped me to write it, and I am grateful to all of them. In particular I would like to thank Tony Collins of Monarch Publications, who first suggested the project, and the many associates of CARE, the Association of Christian Teachers, Christians in Education and the Evangelical Alliance who have patiently responded to my enquiries. Special thanks are due to Mrs Iona Opie who has made her library and her considerable knowledge of English customs and festivals freely available to me. None of the above, of course, should be assumed to agree with the arguments and conclusions of the book. I have also had long conversations with organisations and people whose views on Hallowe'en are very different to mine, for which reason I will not list them here; they have every right to distance themselves from the book's conclusions. I'm grateful, however, for their courtesy and care in explaining their positions to me.

I want to acknowledge two recent books in particular that I have found to be invaluable reference works: David Burnett, *Dawning of the Pagan Moon: An Investigation into the Rise of Western Paganism* (Monarch, 1991), and John Parker, *At the Heart of Darkness: Witchcraft, Black Magic and Satanism Today* (Sidgwick & Jackson, 1993). Though the titles sound similar, the books in fact cover separate topics: the first, by a committed Christian, surveys a broad range of neo-pagan movements; the latter, by an investigative secular journalist, focuses on the explicitly satanic side of occult activity and claims the existence of a highly organised—and highly disturbing—world-wide network of organisations. Both authors have conducted primary research and have interviewed representative figures, though it has to be said that John Parker's factual statements about Christianity and Christian organisations are sometimes inaccurate.

When I drew up the outlines of two earlier books, *Children at Risk* and *Children at Play*, I purposely left Hallowe'en out of the synopses because I knew of the fine work already done in leaflets and discussion papers by Margaret Cooling of the

Association of Christian Teachers. It is a pleasure to acknowledge the generous help and encouragement I have received
from both Margaret and Trevor Cooling in the writing of this
book, as I have fished industriously in a pool they have made
their own.

None of the organisations or individuals who have helped
me, however, are responsible for the opinions and findings
that follow.

*David Porter*
Feast of Good Friday, 1993

CHAPTER ONE

# THE SEASON OF THE WITCH

The boy claws at the mask, but it is stuck to his face like a huge smiling limpet. He moans and dribbles. He is writhing on the floor in front of the television. The television is very loud. If his parents were not watching their son with that fixed, unbelieving horror in their eyes, they would turn it down. But the orchestra goes on playing its ominous crescendo. The composer has matched the tempo with the human heartbeat, filling the air with a sense of dread. The parents watch in horror.

The boy's struggles do not last long, though they seem to go on for ever. Soon he lies still. From the blind mask's mouth, dry rustling spiders emerge and scuttle away like a river of dead flies. Out of one eye socket glides a snake, immensely long and malevolent. The parents' screams threaten to drown the music.

The kids are screaming too—those who are watching at home on video and telly, those who managed to convince the cinema usher that they were older than they were; now they're sitting in pleasurable, spine-tingling excitement as events unfold so realistically, the spiders might be right there in their own living rooms. *Hallowe'en Three: Season of the Witch*, they all agree, has lived up most satisfactorily to the track record of fright and gore established by its celebrated predecessors *Hallowe'en* and *Hallowe'en Two*.

* * *

'Trick or treat! Trick or treat!'

The circle of children press forward excitedly as the front door opens. The lady of the house looks into the pool of dim light. The children are dressed up. Some are wearing pointed hats, some peer out of fearsome masks of wrinkled latex behind which ten-year old giggles are barely concealed. One child holds a lantern made out of a pumpkin slashed with a broad grinning smile illuminated by an electric torch; another wields a broomstick.

'Trick or treat!'

She produces fifty-pence pieces, which the children accept with glee. They would have been satisfied with twenty-pence pieces, but the one with the pumpkin is her son, so she is feeling generous.

Waving cheerfully, they make their way to the next house. The woman closes the door.

'Kids!' she laughs.

In the back room the younger children are having their Hallowe'en party. She's decorated the room for them, all black drapes and silver stars; there are broomsticks and black cats and spooky music on the cassette player. The children have painted their faces and come dressed in witch and demon costumes.

* * *

Bill Jones isn't a kid and hasn't been for a long time. He is thirty-eight and runs a food business in a Manchester suburb. He's a member of the local Chamber of Commerce and does a lot of work for disabled people. He employs three people to whom he is a fair and reasonable boss, just an ordinary bloke if a bit private.

On his way home he drives past the kids tricking and treating and smiles; nice to see them having fun!

He stays home long enough to grab a sandwich and a cup of coffee, then goes out again, carrying a suitcase which he places carefully on the back seat of the car. Inside is a white robe, a silk sash, a curious medallion on a leather thong.

Bill Jones is a witch. Hallowe'en is a special night for him, too.

\* \* \*

Mrs Pagett at the corner shop just hopes that the Hallowe'en stuff will shift. She doesn't want to be stuck with it in November. *Rubber masks and pots of fake gore are all very well but they won't move off the shelves once Hallowe'en is past.* There's a lot of it, too. Magazines like *Fear* and *Scream* have put out their usual bumper Hallowe'en issues. 'The *weirdest* ish ever!' proclaims the American comic, *Tortured Souls*, and a skull with glowing bloodshot eyes stares out at you from the cover. Then there are several boxes of stickers that glow in the dark, a range of amputated fingers with unconvincing imitation blood, some sticky runny slime in sickly green pots, and of course the masks—everything from wrinkled witch faces to crumbling ghouls with shreds of skin hanging from ruined faces. Amazing what you can do with rubber these days . . .

Four-thirty and the schoolkids are in. Lots of noise—*and probably the odd packet of sweets disappearing into pockets that haven't been paid for, but what can you do?* Mrs Pagett shrugs philosophically and organises them into the semblance of a queue. With some satisfaction she sees her stock of Hallowe'en novelties dwindling at a healthy rate as pocket-money follows pocket-money into the till.

\* \* \*

In homes and schools, in village halls and West End cinemas the festival is celebrated, and in some quiet woods and ruined churches too; ducking for apples, ghost stories told by candle-light, disco dancing in gothic twilight, late-night television, old black-and-white horror movies, Boris Karloff, Bela Lugosi, Christopher Lee, Dracula and the Prince of Darkness; the festival of the fires, Samhain, Summerend, All Hallows Eve. Hallowe'en. The Season of the Witch.

Hallowe'en is big business today, quite different in scale and publicity from the days when Ebenezer Brewer included the topic in his 1870 *Dictionary of Phrase and Fable*. Brewer did not even regard it as a festival for the whole of Britain:

> **Hallowe'en** (October 31st), according to Scotch superstition, is the time when witches, devils, fairies and other imps of earth and air hold annual holiday (see *Hallowe'en*, a poem by Robert Burns).[1]

Burns's poem, written almost a century earlier, belongs to the tradition of comic Scots verse of which Burns was the greatest exponent; very much a part of Scots folklore, of only marginal interest to the rest of the world. But in the 1990 *Oxford Current English Dictionary*, Hallowe'en needs little explanation, for it is now part of the Western calendar; the dictionary spends most of its brief space noting the origins of the word.

> **Hallowe'en**, n. 31 Oct., the eve of All Saints' Day (from *hallow* holy person + EVEN).[2]

For many years, Hallowe'en was a domestic festival much like Pancake Tuesday and Bonfire Night; long detached from its historic roots, a chance to have fun and mark the changing seasons.

I remember from my own childhood the various rituals, maybe given more prominence because my sister had a Hallowe'en birthday. There were apples hung from the clothes-rack on strings, to be eaten with your hands tied behind your back; matchsticks that had to be retrieved from piles of flour without using your hands; and many more. Although Hallowe'en was known to have something to do with witches, it was a theme that was marginal and usually ignored in our home—and in many others, to judge by the fact that on Merseyside, where I was brought up, Hallowe'en was usually called 'Duck-Apple Night'. Ducking for apples was yet another game, and one with a very long ancestry. The historian Joseph Strutt mentions that an illustration of the game appears in a fourteenth-century manuscript: he quotes another old author as saying,

> It was customary on the eve of All-Hallows, for the young people in the north to dive for apples, or catch at them when stuck at one end of a kind of hanging beam, at the other extremity of which is fixed a lighted candle, and that with their mouths, only having their hands tied behind their back.[3]

For many writers both ancient and modern the Hallowe'en games are intriguing reminders of historic titbits now forgotten and irrelevant, just as nursery rhymes often contain specific allusions to events in the past, and the names of the days of the week embody the pantheon of Viking gods.

True, among the traditional entertainments is a strong emphasis on what Iona and Peter Opie describe as 'divination':

> Hallowe'en, [the children] well know, is the night above all others when supernatural influences prevail, the night when divinations are most likely to succeed.[4]

It is the night for brushing your hair three times in front of a mirror, so that your future husband will appear in the mirror behind you; for tossing apple-peel over your shoulder so that it will form his initials as it falls. The Opies record the tradition that the initials can also be obtained by keeping two snails in a box over Hallowe'en night; by morning they will have traced the initials in silvery slime.

But even comparatively recently there was a kind of innocence about the festival. You tried to find out the initials of your future husband but you cast no charms to make him love you despite himself. The games gave a lot of amusement to the bystanders watching the antics of those struggling to bite the bobbing apple, but anyone who succeeded was allowed to keep the apple. The association with witchcraft was acknowledged, but who knew a witch? For most of us, witches both black and white were comfortably in the realm of the unlikely and unlooked-for.

Today it's quite different. Hallowe'en has become a major industry, and for a significant minority the festival is anything but innocent. As we shall see in this book, it never really was a trivial festival; although thousands celebrated it unthinkingly, for many it was always a night of the greatest possible significance.

Superficially, however, the triviality is still to the fore. You won't find greengrocers today advertising cheap apples for Duck-Apple Night, but you'll find all the trappings of synthetic horror and Hollywood witchcraft, and your local newsagent will have a range of suitably blood-curdling magazines and comics. The local cinema will probably be showing a horror film. Discos will advertise Vampire nights, the high street video library will be clean out of Hallowe'en and other horror videos, and there will be features on TV and radio.

For many people the first problems encountered with Hallowe'en are as parents. Hallowe'en is used in many schools as the opportunity to capitalise on the child's already stimulated imagination and harness it to educational purposes. Its rich resource of fantasy and intrinsic fascination (children are inveterate dalliers with the bizarre and spooky) has brought Hallowe'en projects into many syllabuses at both primary and secondary level. Parents often have reservations about this, ranging from religious objections (many faiths find frivolous exploration of the occult deeply offensive) to an unwillingness to deal with the nightmares that can result from Hallowe'en games that are too boisterous, or class projects that become too involving for some children.

But concern over Hallowe'en is being expressed by people in many different situations and from many different backgrounds, worried about the impact of the festival on people of all ages. The argument extends far beyond the festival itself and addresses the matter of the context of Hallowe'en—a very different context to that in which Hallowe'en existed even thirty or forty years ago. What was once an event Christianised into the calendar of a country that could (in some respects at least) be called a Christian country—and renamed the Eve of

All Hallows—has been transformed into a festival of pagan origins celebrated in a country that in some respects has reverted to its pagan roots.[5]

In this new context, there is concern about Hallowe'en from those to whom it is a significant festival, a high point in their calendar; the growing number of practising witches, occultists, satanists and other worshippers in the neo-pagan revival. For them, the festival is a pale mockery of the past, reduced to childhood games and frivolity. But even these remnants, they recognise, serve to illustrate the continuity of pagan themes of life and death.[6]

By contrast, at least one significant writer on children sees Hallowe'en as a basically healthy holiday that has been stripped of its vitality by interfering modern adults. Bruno Bettelheim, whose book *A Good Enough Parent* (1987) has had a wide influence for its many valuable insights, writes from the American perspective:

> Although in the United States we have no children's holiday [like St Nicholas' Day in Holland] which centers so clearly and delight-fully on ambivalence, we used to have one which ritually celebrated and discharged the negative component of children's ambivalence about the world of adults: Halloween . . . Children could act out their resentments of those adults who all year long expected them to act more civilized than they wanted or were able to be.[7]

It was 'the one day when they could threaten adults, as they feel threatened by them all year round, and scare them, as they are scared by adults'. Adults, comments Bettelheim, used to collaborate in the fun by acting scared and 'buying off the child's threats by giving him goodies in response to his demand of "trick or treat".' Bettelheim sees Hallowe'en as an opportunity to master aggressive desires:

> Christmas symbolizes the satisfaction of all our hopes, but Halloween symbolizes our persecutory anxieties. The witch on her broomstick . . . is the reincarnation of the bad mother, the hostile-destructive one. The devil, a figure which in every way symbolizes

phallic aggression (the hoof, the tail, the horns), represents the bad father . . . Before Halloween was bowdlerized, children were able to attain power for one night.

For Bettelheim the festival has degenerated into a fancy-dress party, and the symbolism has become 'demystified and civilized', even being used as the occasion for collections for UNICEF. Bettelheim, arguing as he does in the case of several other issues in the book, maintains that denying the child fulfilment in this way may create angry, resentful individuals later on who will hate adults.

What is extraordinary in Bruno Bettelheim's discussion of Hallowe'en is not his attitude to the festival but the fact that in 1987 he was able to write of a festival of witch lore without reference to the burgeoning interest in the occult. By 1987 a large number of witchcraft organisations and other pagan societies were in operation and John Carpenter's three Hallowe'en films had been made, which certainly do not celebrate the victory of children over adults, in fact quite the reverse. Yet Bettelheim does not choose to make any connection between the fantasy celebrations of the popular children's festival and the real celebrations which others regard as valid. He treats as meaningless play, symbols that thousands across the modern West take as full of meaning.

He represents one extreme in a debate about Hallowe'en that has grown considerably in recent years, partly because a number of Christian organisations have published objections and partly because the festival itself has become much more prominent as the West moves further into a 'post-Christian' society and paganism becomes both more widely established and socially acceptable.

In television programmes like *Donahue* and *The Oprah Winfrey Show*, practising witches, occultists and New Age spokesmen and spokeswomen are given a platform. They are listened to with great attention by studio audiences of ordinary men and women who apparently don't consider it at all strange to be listening, along with a TV audience of several million, to speakers who acknowledge the authority of voices from the grave, spirit guides, and sometimes explicitly satanic forces. Oprah Winfrey (who is a rich and powerful advocate of the New Age) is seen on British television at five o'clock in the evening, well within the time period allocated to general family viewing.

Is this a problem?

In one sense, it is not, at least in that there is nothing sinister in it. The media have an insatiable appetite for the new, the exotic, the bizarre; and the mood of this post-Christian age lends any discussion of the supernatural a particular appeal. As G.K. Chesterton is said to have remarked, when people stop believing in God, they do not then believe in nothing, they believe in anything. In Christian terms, there is a spiritual void in human beings that demands to be filled, and those who offer spiritual goods find ready buyers. Television has no brief to be a missionary society for the Christian faith, however much I and my fellow-Christians (and arguably its founding fathers) may wish it to be. It reflects our society and sometimes shapes it, but it does not do so as an act of Christian evangelism.

In another sense, it is a problem, for it would be naive to assume that everybody who speaks on television as spokesperson for occult religions, the New Age gospel and other modern religious movements is presenting a straightforward account of themselves. The history of witchcraft in Britain contains plenty of brilliant manipulators of the media who successfully hoodwinked the public as to their real agenda, often by playing along with the popular concept of how they, as witches, should be behaving while at the same time engaging in practices that the public would have been horrified to have known about. If there are hidden agendas among occult practitioners today, it is certain that they are not mentioned on television chat shows.

It's a complex issue. In this book I shall be assuming that the spectrum of pagan and satanic belief in the West today includes a large number of believers who have embraced paganism as a personal faith. It would be helpful, indeed, if Christians anxious to develop outreach to other religions would accept many of these movements as religions in the same way as Islam, Buddhism and others are accepted, rather than equating them with devil-worship and horrific practices. Not all are.

On the other hand—many are; though perhaps not as many as William Schnoebelen, an ex-wicca high priest, would claim. He sees all witches of any persuasion and virtually all pagans as being on an inexorable path to satanism, and claims that churches such as Anton LaVey's Church of Satan (which we shall be discussing in Chapter 5) are laughable fronts for the rampant satanism that flourishes independently of such high-profile operations.[8]

Yet with the high profile of pagan belief in our times—whether it be as a new religious movement comparable to others such as humanism and many more, or as a much darker manifestation of the occult quest and even devotion to Satan —an uneasy feeling seems to be growing among many who would not think of themselves as religious at all, that the trappings, customs and associations of the ancient festival of Hallowe'en have a reality that has not faded over the centuries. Indeed, it may sometimes appear that the deeper meanings of Hallowe'en belong to a belief system whose time has come again.

## CHAPTER TWO

# HALLOWTIDE

The terrified policeman, stripped of his uniform and dressed in a white, shroud-like gown, is dragged to the headland followed by a straggling crowd of celebrants decked in flower headresses, animal masks and strange ritual garments. As they clear the dunes at the cliff's edge a weird and horrifying spectacle comes into view: a huge wicker statue in the shape of a giant, looming twenty feet or more into the twilit sky, inside which hens and other livestock peer out from their flower-decked prison clucking miserably. High in the giant's abdomen a rough door is open ready. The ladder up to the door rises out of piles of faggots and kindling laid ready at the monster's base: nearby, people stand ready with flickering torches, waiting for the signal to set the whole thing ablaze. The policeman takes in the scene at a glance, screams in pure terror, then appears to relapse into a trance, sleepwalking the last few yards, reciting the Lord's prayer in a defiant, dogged voice though he knows all hope is gone. The wicker man will claim his victim once again.

The above is not a fanciful and somewhat lurid retelling of pagan myths. It is a description of the closing moments of a film made by Robin Hardy in 1973, *The Wicker Man*. While I have attempted to capture in words the power of Hardy's images, nothing can convey the brooding, malevolent evil that permeates the film, most effectively because much of the tragedy revolves around the apparent innocence of children turning out to be a cloak for extreme wickedness (a factor which caused a recent showing of the film on British television to be postponed, as the Commission on the Orkney child abuse allegations was due to present an interim report that week: it was felt that the theme of the film might be seen as a vindication of the accusations of ritual abuse).

*The Wicker Man* is set in modern times. The macabre plot involves a policeman arriving in a remote Scottish island ruled by a practising pagan lord, to investigate the disappearance of a child. He finds a society dedicated to the worship of pagan deities and claiming a continuity with pagan observances from long before Christianity. The policeman, a practising Christian, is appalled by what he finds, and unsuccessfully tries to confront local children with the basic facts of Christianity: these are ridiculed and considered irrelevant on the island.

Approached by a seductive local girl in his lodgings he resists her advances because he intends to remain a virgin until marriage. In this he reveals himself to be the perfect sacrifice: sexually pure, gullible and coming of his own choice to the island. The film ends with his discovery that the 'missing child' was a plot to lure a sacrificial victim to the island. He is dragged to the headland in the manner described above, and the final credits of the film roll across a darkening sky, as the last of the sun drops into the sea and the smoke and leaping flames of the sacrifice form a pagan lighthouse across the tranquil sea.

The film's theme, though embellished with fantasy and drawing upon a number of religious traditions and themes, is by no means a fiction. By that I do not mean, of course, that one should today expect to find satanic abuse of children in remote Scottish islands more than one should expect to find such abuse anywhere else. Hardy has simply presented his viewers with a reconstruction of rituals known to have been practised in ancient European Celtic communities and preserved in folk memory: the fire festivals.

Hallowe'en today is part of a trilogy of celebrations: Hallowe'en, or All Hallow's Eve (observed on 31 October), All Saints' Day (celebrated on 1 November), and All Souls'

Day (celebrated on 2 November). Of these the second and third (sometimes referred to together as 'Hallowtide') are festivals created by the Christian church. Hallowe'en, however, is a festival whose roots are deep in pre-Christian religion and which in modern times retains much of its pagan symbolism.

In Celtic religion, for example, Hallowe'en was a major focal point in the cycle of fire festivals which *The Wicker Man* reflects. Sir James Frazer, the author of a massive, learned (and sometimes unreliable) anthropological study *The Golden Bough*, collected a large number of accounts of such festivals from all over Europe.[1] Frazer's findings comprise a disturbing catalogue. He considered that the theme of human sacrifice clearly survived in many of the festivals he records: for example, in second-century Gaul a huge human figure was constructed out of a wicker-work of branches and vegetation, and human beings were burned alive inside them together with various livestock (the Celts used the occasion as an opportunity of executing condemned criminals). This festival, which took place every fifth year, was a fertility rite, just as it was in Hardy's imaginative film reconstruction.

Frazer described many much more recent fire rituals involving the sacrifice of hens and animals in wicker-work images.

In the Central Highlands of Scotland bonfires, known as the Beltane fires, were formerly kindled with great ceremony on the first of May, and the traces of human sacrifices at them were particularly clear and unequivocal . . . [John Ramsay, a friend of Sir Walter Scott, wrote of more modern survivals:] 'Like the other public worship of the Druids, the Beltane feast seems to have been performed on hills or eminences. They thought it degrading to him whose temple is the universe, to suppose that he would dwell in any house made with hands. Their sacrifices were therefore offered in the open air, frequently on the tops of hills, where they were presented with the grandest views of nature, and were nearest the seat of warmth and order.'

Frazer quotes many examples, gathered by himself and others, of observances of fire festivals and sacrifices in places all over Europe and at historical periods ranging from ancient history to modern times.

The continental fire festivals usually took place at the solstices: the most important European fire festival, Frazer suggests, was the one celebrating Midsummer's Eve. There was a link between worshipping pagan earth forces and the moments in the calendar when those forces were clearly at their most powerful—the sun being then highest in the sky, the day at its longest.

The Celts of the British Isles, however, arranged their fire-festivals without reference to the cosmic calendar.[2] They observed two festivals: the May Beltane fires, and the October festival at Hallowe'en. The Beltane fires marked the onset of summer, and Hallowe'en that of winter—'The last night of October . . . when the Celtic peoples celebrated 'Winter's Eve' and the beginning of their New Year.'[3] Hallowe'en, as the mark of the end of the year, was a common feature of the festival in several parts of the British Isles: in the Isle of Man for example mummers used to chant a song in Old Manx: 'Tonight is New Year's Night'. In ancient Ireland, a sacred fire was kindled from which all other sacred flames were to be kindled throughout the year to come. Frazer writes:

> Another confirmation of the view that the Celts dated their year from the first of November is furnished by the manifold modes of divination which were commonly resorted to by Celtic people for the purpose of ascertaining their destiny . . . for when could these devices for prying into the future be more reasonably put into practice than at the beginning of the year?[4]

Central to the festival of Hallowe'en was the celebration of the dead. The Celtic New Year festival was known as the celebration of Samhain, the Lord of the Dead. The eve of November 1st, the day on which the old year died, was a very appropriate time to honour death.

The Druids regarded Hallowe'en as a particularly sacred time. Modern Druids still do:

The Druid rites . . . were concerned with making contact with the spirits of the departed, who were seen as sources of guidance and inspiration rather than as sources of dread . . . The dead are honoured and feasted, not as the dead, but as the living spirits of loved ones and of guardians who hold the root-wisdom of the tribe.[5]

This is the opinion of Philip Carr-Gomm, a leading modern-day Druid. He is dismissive of the gorier aspects of early druidic history, but it's a theme that recurs in most writings on the subject. T.D. Kendrick for example, in a classic work on Druidism, acknowledges that 'the Irish historian, Dr. Geoffrey Keating, who was born in the 16th century, speaks of druidic sacrifice on the occasion of the Samhain bonfire.'[6]

Witchcraft, too, sees Hallowe'en as a great night. Sally, a witch queen of Kent, says:

I love Halloween. I think I'm a very autumn person. We dress up the house with cobwebs and so on and we cast a circle, and we have a smokey cauldron and we all scry—which means do clairvoyance, into the smoke which comes out of the cauldron—and we open the gates of the underworld and if any spirits want to come forward and speak, we listen to them.

Another British witch recalls,

My first initiation when I became first degree was on Hallowe'en, and I felt very very much in tune with the god.[7]

However much the trappings of broomsticks, cauldrons, masks and other paraphernalia may be trivialised by commercial interests and the media, in this context they have a reality and an energy that is by no means trivial.

For the Christian church, Hallowe'en in this sense represents spiritual warfare of the most explicit kind. Confrontation with Hallowe'en could only be a matter of time for the emerging Christian church in the early centuries of Christendom.

## The Church's initiative

*Hallowtide*

The young Christian church, as it spread outwards from its beginnings in the Holy Land, across Europe and further across the whole world, came into contact with other religions and their customs. Some of those customs involved human and animal sacrifice; some involved explicit belief in, and worship of, gods and goddesses incompatible with worship of the God of the Bible; and some celebrated values and phenomena which the church did not oppose or deny, but which were in pagan worship placed into a quite different context and system of beliefs to that which Christianity taught.

Where necessary the church tried to stamp out cruelty; human sacrifice, for example, was something that was strongly opposed. Worship of other gods was often countered by destruction of the images and temples. In many other cases, however, the church simply produced its own rival product, in effect baptising the old. When a country was converted to Christianity the new celebrations took the place of the old, at least so far as the majority of the population was concerned. The same was true of many other aspects of the old religions: for example, archaeologists have discovered pagan artefacts and styles of church furnishings that have been given new, Christian meanings: for example,

> a find of Christian silver from Water Newton, Huntingdonshire, now in the British Museum. The treasure includes a number of triangular plaques resembling pagan votive offerings but stamped with Christian symbols . . . a silver bowl inscribed 'I Publianus, humbly trusting in you Lord, honour your holy altar.'[8]

The same often applied to festivals:

> Christians 'took over' festivals of these pre-Christian religions and changed their meaning, so that they became times for celebrating particular aspects of Christian belief. For example, Christmas customs involving lights and candles were originally connected

with an ancient midwinter festival in which people tried to persuade the sun to return for another summer. Christians changed the meaning so that the lights became symbols of Jesus, who described himself as the Light of the World.[9]

One pre-Christian festival that presented a particular challenge to the Christian church was Hallowe'en, with its violent history and its veneration of earth deities and times and seasons. And as the church progressed, the Christian Hallowtide festivals came into existence as a new alternative and counter to the old ways.

## All Saints' Day

All Saints' Day has its origins in the third century, and was at first celebrated in mid-May. It became a major event in the Christian calendar in the early sixth century, when Pope Boniface IV consecrated the old Pantheon in Rome to become a Christian church (the Pantheon was a splendid building built just before the birth of Christ, the interior of which contained niches decorated with statues of various gods; Boniface's dedication of it as a church was therefore a good example of the 'baptism' of pagan artefacts discussed above.)

From then on, a commemoration of 'All Saints' was held annually. In the century following the consecration of the Pantheon, a chapel to 'All the Saints' was dedicated in the basilica of St Peter on 1 November, and the yearly festival of All Saints was moved to that date.

As the centuries went by, the number of people regarded as 'Saints' by the church grew, and so did the number of patron saints and saints given special reverence by particular groups. Throughout the year many saints' days were observed, but it became increasingly useful to have the 'catch-all' festival at the beginning of November, in which all saints, including those who did not have a special day of their own, could be remembered. The church has traditionally regarded it as a festival to honour all saints 'known and unknown'.

In the 1662 *Book of Common Prayer*, the collect for All Saints' Day reads as follows:

O Almighty God, who hast knit together thine elect in one communion and fellowship, in the mystical body of thy son Christ our Lord: Grant us peace so to follow thy blessed Saints in all virtuous and godly living, that we may come to those unspeakable joys, which thou hast prepared for them that unfeignedly love thee; through Jesus Christ our Lord.

The Epistle for All Saints' Day is from Revelation 7 (the 'great multitude, which no man could number'); the Gospel is from Matthew 5, referring to the example of courage and spirituality of those Christians who have died before us. 'This festival,' explains one writer, 'is a continuation of the early commemoration of martyrs, too numerous for individual commemoration; later, all dead Christians were included.'[10]

The theme of All Saints' Day is well expressed in the hymn that is often sung then:

For all the Saints, who from their labours rest
Who thee by faith before the world confessed,
Thy name, O Jesus, be for ever blessed.
  Hallelujah! Hallelujah! . . .

From earth's wide bounds, from ocean's farthest coast,
Through gates of pearl streams in the countless host,
Singing to Father, Son and Holy Ghost—
  Hallelujah! Hallelujah!

(*William Walsham How*)

Bishop How (1823–1897) wrote the hymn as a processional for All Saints' Day, though it is sung at other times as well.

## All Souls' Day

The Feast of All Souls is not observed today in all churches. One reason in many Protestant churches is the implied distinction between the 'saints' of the previous day's feast and the 'souls' of All Souls' Day, which is thought to teach a doctrine of purgatory and a two-tier view of the after-life which those churches reject. A second reason is that All Souls' Day, unlike All Saints' Day, has prompted many echoes and survivals of the old pagan customs in the practices and traditions that surround it.

The festival began as a local celebration in Cluny in Burgundy, France. Odilo, the influential abbot of the Cluny monastery, instituted 2 November (or 3 November, if 2 November fell on a Sunday) as an annual celebration to commemorate the souls of the Christian dead and to pray for the 'faithful departed'. He instructed all the Benedictine monasteries under his jurisdiction to observe the new festival, but it was not long before it was celebrated throughout the whole Christian church.

In various parts of Britain, traditional customs preserve the pre-Christian significance of Hallowtide. The pagan belief that the dead walked on one night of the year sat easily in folk tradition with the desire to honour and perhaps placate the dead.

> Many continued in the Celtic belief that for one night the souls of the dead could visit them, and taste earthly food once again. There was a custom of preparing a meal on All Souls' Eve and leaving the door open overnight so that the dead souls could enter and eat. The meal consisted of wine and little cakes called 'soul-cakes'.[11]

In some areas even today the tradition of 'souling' continues, which began as the custom of begging special cakes for the dead; as Antony Ewens points out, under Christian influence this changed to the custom of wealthy people giving 'soul-cakes' to the poor. Eventually this too changed, and the 'Soulers' were given fruit, beer, sweets or money.

Like many customs from ancient times, souling today has often become a children's custom. Iona and Peter Opie, in their collection of children's sayings, record several souling songs: for example,

My Souling Cap, my Souling Cap,
It cost me many a shilling,
My shoes are wore out through tramping about,
And I can't get a pint of beer.

'Soul-cakes are no longer made,' wrote the Opies in 1959, 'and the children are usually rewarded with apples, biscuits or coins which, however, they may stoutly refer to as 'soul-cakes'.' They quote an interesting song that well illustrates how closely pagan and Christian themes can become intertwined in folk-lore:

> Soul! Soul! for a soul-cake!
> I pray you, good missis, a soul-cake!
> An apple, a pear, a plum or a cherry,
> Or any good thing to make us all merry.
> One for Peter, two for Paul,
> Three for Them that made us all.[12]

## The pagan survival

The church fought vigorously against the survival of pre-Christian festivities such as the fire festivals; in the eighth century, the church synods attempted to abolish them because they were pagan rituals.

However, the folk customs did not die easily. The old practices of human sacrifice largely disappeared, and though the fires were still lit, dummies replaced the human victims. In mediaeval times, when witches (real and supposed) were persecuted, they were executed at the stake and their effigies were often thrown on the Hallowe'en fires. When in 1605 Guy Fawkes led a conspiracy to blow up the king and parliament, it became the custom to light the autumn fire on 5 November instead of 31 October, and it was his effigy that was burned.

The use of lights to frighten off evil spirits, so much a part of the old festival, continued in village festivals in various parts of Britain. In modern times, a turnip-lantern ('punkie') procession is held in Hinton St George in Somerset on the fourth Thursday in October: a children's chant is sung as follows—

> It's Punkie Night tonight,
> It's Punkie Night tonight,
> Give us a candle, give us a light,
> If you don't you'll get a fright.

The words, of course, recall the purpose of the original fires, as does the practice, still observed in Ottery St Mary in Devon, of rolling burning tar barrels down the high street. Customs recalling Celtic beliefs—such as leaving food out for the dead to eat when they came back to earth on All Souls' night—continued too, and the custom of collecting 'pennies for the guy' in the days before Bonfire Night draws both upon the custom of souling or 'guising' and also the traditional early November 'mischief nights'—a reflection of the lawlessness and chaos that was part of the original Hallowe'en.

Such customs are pagan survivals, but they are corrupted memories. They do not constitute a living pagan tradition (such a tradition certainly exists, but these are not part of it). In modern times, when the quality of community life is often deteriorating and urban and rural identity is harder to preserve, such customs can play an important part in building social interaction and community involvement.

They are, I would suggest, the attractive face of the old beliefs. Usually cherished by children rather than adults, they look back to a world that seems in hindsight more attractive than it in reality was. Few people would want to abolish them, and for most they represent a world they would not want to lose.

Yet there are much stronger survivals in modern Hallowtide. Ancient rituals are being recited today much as they were a thousand years ago, and gods and spirits are being worshipped who were worshipped in the West before the birth of Christ. Some groups actively worship the devil; others (the majority, in fact) claim to repudiate satanism and to devote themselves to caring for the planet and for their fellow human beings. Some regard Christianity as a recent religion, of little enduring worth; some regard themselves as in amiable co-existence with Christianity; others hate Christianity and would destroy it if they could.

For all these, Hallowe'en is a special occasion in a way that other traditional festivals are not. We shall go on to look at some of these groupings, and some of the ways in which the Hallowe'en themes are emphasised in our modern society. But first we must look at what might be called the 'secular view' of Hallowe'en—the view that the whole affair is now so wrapped up in antiquity that it is meaningless, a convenient package of resources to tickle our imaginations and chill our spines, but in terms of anything that actually matters, a piece of harmless fiction and a trivial legend.

## CHAPTER THREE

# THE SECULAR VIEW

The devil? Oh, he's not real, he's just like Santa Claus.
He's just your father dressed up.
*(Comment ascribed to a primary school pupil)*

When Mr and Mrs Average and family decorate their home
for Hallowe'en and they or their children embark upon the
annual traditions, they are drawing on a rich heritage of
ancient customs and practices. There are very few aspects of
modern Hallowe'en observances that date from recent times,
and most date from the pre-Christian era. Hallowe'en is one
of the oldest of our calendar festivals.

The question is—does it really matter? After all, many
events in the calendar reflect ancient history, and some
celebrate quite gory matters: Bonfire Night, for example, is a
reminder of an attempt at arson on the grand scale and the
attempted massacre of the entire House of Commons. But
antiquity has a distancing, sanitising effect. One of my hobbies
is military board wargaming; I might spend an interesting
evening recreating Alexander the Great's strategy in the
Battle of Arbela on my computer, but would have no interest
at all in recreating the Falklands War campaign in which
people living near me fought and died, and in which individuals
I have met lived in a state of siege under heavy bombardment.
To quote an old wargaming proverb, cardboard soldiers don't
bleed; and neither do twopenny guy-fawkeses. Does anybody
seriously argue that celebrating Bonfire Night will prompt an

unhealthy interest in arson and regicide? It all happened so long ago, the significance of the festival is long forgotten by most of us.

Yet an increasing number of people *are* expressing concern about Hallowe'en. One of the main areas of concern is in education, for schools have often used the festival as the opportunity for creative play and teaching a variety of topics. The concern has been noted by the teaching profession: in the *Times Educational Supplement* in 1992, a week before Hallowe'en, author Heather Sharpe introduced an article as follows:

> Many teachers are worried about telling tales of the supernatural. And if they're not worried themselves, they're worried about parents who might be. These anxieties, raised in many in-service sessions on storytelling, have intensified following the efforts of certain groups to put an Act through Parliament banning the celebration of Hallowe'en in schools. Objections fall into two categories: first, pupils may be unduly frightened or disturbed; second, they might be encouraged to 'dabble in the occult' and thus be led into physical and spiritual danger.[1]

The concern had been expressed for some time, not least by sections of the teaching profession itself. In March 1986 the Inner London Education Authory Inspectorate distributed a document that began as follows:

*ILEA Inspectors' Warning on Occultism in Schools*

To: Head Teachers in all Schools March 1986

Dear Colleague,

The Education Officer receives a small but continuous stream of letters from parents who are concerned that their children's interest in the occult is being stimulated by aspects of their education. This may involve reading schemes which involve ghosts, teaching about witches, computer games with a strong 'fear' element, celebration of Hallowe'en and direct teaching about the occult. Something of the anxiety of parents may be gauged by the fact that a Christian organisation has just published and completely sold 50,000 copies of a pamphlet called *Danger Children at Play* within four weeks.

We have therefore met as an Inspectorate Committee to consider the matter and believe it would be helpful if we registered our concerns so that you may bear them in mind when deciding on your own policies . . .

The response of many teachers to such presentations was one of polite bemusement. Why should there be concern over what was essentially a folk festival, offering rich possibilities for imaginative class projects, investigation into legend and tradition, images and drama galore? Surely Hallowe'en was no more than a harmless fantasy, drawing on a common stock of forgotten stories, of no more consequence than the fairy stories and comics that have been the staple reading of children and teenagers for many years?

Parents who registered concern, even when that concern was expressed quietly and courteously (not all parents expressed it thus) sometimes found themselves categorised as 'fundamentalists', marginalised as cranks and troublemakers.

But the concern was already widespread even in 1986. When, back in 1982, the Association of Christian Teachers had published a four-page leaflet *Hallowe'en*—a brief, considered and non-contentious summary of the main concerns being expressed—the document received considerable press and media coverage, though the Association pointed out that it was merely making the leaflet available as part of its services to teachers, and that many other leaflets on a wide range of topics had been published that year.

It was a reflection of the growing popular interest in the debate that in October 1989 I was invited by BBC Radio Cardiff to take part in a debate about Hallowe'en. The other participant in the discussion was John Gilbert, who was at that time the editor of the recently-launched glossy magazine *Fear*. I enjoyed the meeting, the discussion and the conversation afterwards that went on between us for some considerable time after the formal debate was over. In his editorial in the next issue of the magazine Mr Gilbert mentioned the occasion and commented on the opposition of certain evangelical Christian and other pressure groups to the festival of Hallowe'en. I quote extensively from his comments below, partly because I discussed with him at length the topic they cover, and partly because they seem to me to be to be a fair summary of what might be called the 'secular' view of Hallowe'en, conceding neither the Christian nor the pagan case.

### Real Horror Behind Hallowe'en

Just before Hallowe'en I appeared on a BBC radio programme which explored the [Hallowe'en] controversy. Fortunately, the show was well balanced, the interviewer clued-up on the subject and the gentleman I was supposedly pitted against willing to be involved in a critical argument. There are, however, some groups who are so obsessed with their own righteousness that they cannot see the hypocrisy in what they say. Since they persist in mentioning horror and fantasy in the same holier-than-thou breath as Hallowe'en, perhaps it's about time that someone fed them a few truths.

Hallowe'en has nothing to do with good or evil. Once a pagan festival in celebration and remembrance of the dead, wound in—like most pagan rituals—with fertility worship of the Earth Mother Goddess, Hallowe'en is centred around the life principle—no stereotypical witches, demons and devils.

Like so many successful religions before (and after) it, Christianity absorbed and transmogrified most pagan rituals and holy days including Hallowe'en. To hallow is to make holy, and the Church festival is All Hallows Eve, or All Saints Day. Nevertheless, as with Christmas, the common people continued to observe the underside of the Christian holy day and it was the Church which introduced the popular witchy feeling to the commoners' festival. The old gods became the new demons, and you can see some of the pagan deities within the faces of gargoyles and even the Devil himself.

Who, then, was originally responsible for Hallowe'en which is now, admittedly, a disgustingly commercial venture? Why, the early Christians, and it can be historically proved. Today it's the

Americans. If we in Britain are to be concerned about the rise in popularity of Hallowe'en, we should look to the States. Hallowe'en, though never entirely absent, has hardly, in recent times, enjoyed the recognition it has always had in America . . . until very recently. Images from movies like *Halloween*, even more saintly films such as *E.T.*, have begun having a commercial effect in the UK. It's an opportunity to sell masks, costumes and—who knows before long—fancy cards.

I'm certainly no pagan but the moral majority is about to squirm even further when I say that Christmas—you know, the jolly season we're about to celebrate—was, also a pagan festival. The Christmas tree is a pagan symbol, so are Yuletide logs, as are the baubles and candles; and what earthy spirits are to be found hiding behind pretty symbols like holly, ivy and (kissing under the) mistletoe?

Now, I'm in no way taking a sideways swipe at those people who think that everything is evil unless it fits in with their conception of god [*sic*]—I happen to be fairly moderate in my views when compared to some people in the fantasy genre. Like so many people who can distinguish between fact and fantasy—and who like to get their facts right—I am fed up with people who constantly draw an illogical connection between horror and the occult and who seem to have nothing better to do than make ordinary people, who happen to write about the fantastic, into slavering perverts ready to turn the world toward some devil.[3]

The words 'Hallowe'en has nothing to do with good or evil' are highly significant, for neither the Christian nor the pagan would accept that statement at all, though their categories and definitions would differ markedly. Yet it is a common position held by many who publish, and who consume, fantasy and horror entertainment. It rejects the existence of a personal devil, and treats all horror stories as being harmless—if scary—entertainment; speculation about nothing, a playing around with a concept that is totally imaginary.[4]

A correspondent in the letters page of the British fantasy role-playing game magazine *G. M.* in 1989 summed up the argument succinctly:

I would like to express my views on the so called connection between *D&D* [Dungeons and Dragons] and the occult. Personally I believe the connection is a load of old bull and if people in the 20th century still believe in witches, then they will be campaigning for the return of the ducking stool next!

Why don't these people pull their heads out of the clouds and realise that this is 1989 and not the 1500s. Are they so scared of history and their own imaginations that they can't tell the difference between a game and a religion?[5]

This reader's letter raises two questions which we will be considering again in this book. The first, as to whether witches still exist in the twentieth century, is an easy one to answer. Any of the three leading British organisations of witches (The Pagan Federation, PaganLink or The Green Circle) would no doubt have been happy to send him further details: they are not secret organisations but on the contrary are very happy to receive publicity. The second question, as to whether a game could be considered harmful, is certainly one that many teachers and parents would have an opinion on as relating to Hallowe'en; at the very least, the highly graphic portrayals of occult paraphernalia and witchcraft in many schools have often resulted in children being very disturbed at home and taking several days to get over their nervousness at returning to their elaborately-decorated classroom. Even if one considers the occult to be an outdated, meaningless folk memory of more religious days, it is still questionable whether fantasising about such things is a helpful pastime.

But the secular view of Hallowe'en and the supernatural is only one among several views. In this book we shall see that for an increasing number of people, from various backgrounds and of various faiths, Hallowe'en is anything *but* imaginary. For some it is a disturbing evocation of forces and beliefs that resonate with a dark, occult view of the supernatural world. For others it is a celebration of life forces, a celebration of good in a context of legalised chaos, the night when normal spiritual categories are set aside. For some it is a celebration of values to which they find themselves deeply opposed; for others it is an opportunity to affirm allegiance and faith towards those same values. For none of these groups is Hallowe'en other than a night deeply concerned with good and evil.

## Christmas—a pagan tradition?

The case argued by John Gilbert that Hallowe'en's present form is the creation of the Christian church is often put forward, and the association of various non-Christian elements of Christmas celebration—yule logs, Christmas trees, the druidic mistletoe etc.—with the Christian festival of the Christ-child is one often made when discussions take place about Hallowe'en. But there is no real comparison between the two festivals.

Let's look at Mr Gilbert's comments about Christmas a little more closely. He is quite right to draw attention to the pagan origins of much of the paraphernalia of Christmas. Most of it comes originally from Scandinavia, and is taken from pre-Christian festivals of the winter solstice (traditionally, under the modern calendar, taken to be 25 December).

Thus *Christmas trees* have their origins in the legendary Scandinavian ash-tree, Yggdrasil—the Tree of Time. Its roots penetrated to other realms, including Helheim, the home of the dead. Christmas tree *decorations* originate in the ancient Roman December festival of Saturn, when the temple was decorated with greenery. In Scandinavia, the holly tree was popular for the same reason that it is a familiar part of British Christmas celebrations; it is a plant that produces both foliage and fruit in the middle of winter. *Kissing under the mistletoe* is a kind of preventive ritual—it was an arrow made of mistletoe that slew the Scandinavian god Baldr. Baldr came back to life, and the mistletoe was put under the care of the goddess Frigg; it would never be a tool of evil again until it touched the earth. Hence in decoration it is always hung from the ceiling, and the custom of kissing beneath it was an affirmation that this particular evil no longer had any power.

The *Yule log* is not seen very much today but is a familiar part of the tradition of Christmas, still to be found on Christmas card scenes if nowhere else. It was a huge log laid across the hearth on Christmas Eve, and there were many ceremonies and celebrations associated with it: this, too, has links with Scandinavia, as can be seen from the name itself; for example, the Old Norse *jól* (Yule) referred to the mid-winter pagan festival and was later applied to Christmas. From this word, compounds such as *jól-drykkja* (Yule-drinking) and *jól-veizla* (Yule-banquet) were formed, indicating that both Yule and Christmas were highly significant times in Scandinavian life.

All this might seem to endorse Mr Gilbert's point that 'Christmas is a pagan festival', especially when one finds that Yuletide, the time of the Winter solstice, and the date of 25 December have all been held as sacred festivals for many groups in many countries. For Christians, 25 December is the anniversary of the birth of Jesus Christ. Chinese Buddhism regards 25 December as the birth-date of Buddha, son of Maya. The Druids observe 22 December, the winter solstice, as the ceremony of Alban Arthuan, the celebration of death and rebirth. In Egypt, the god Horus was believed to have been born at the end of December, and in Greece several gods and goddesses were believed to have been born at the winter solstice. In India it is a time of religious festivals, in Mexico the solstice was the occasion for festivals in honour of the rain god Tlalocs, in Scandinavia Freya was honoured at Yuletide. In ancient Persia the sun-god Mithras was held to have been born on 25 December, and in ancient Rome the Saturnalia was celebrated in mid-December, and on 25 December itself the festival of *Natalis Solis Invicta*—'the birth of the unconquered sun'.

Does this mean that the Christian festival of Christmas is therefore riddled with pagan belief, sharing a common fascination with the solstice and a desire to reverence the earth-forces and the gods of nature and rebirth? Is Christmas, in fact, a collection of pagan oddments bolted on to an essentially Christian celebration, much as many of the religions referred to above created their own December festivals? Some Christian groups, both in the past and in the present day, have refused to celebrate Christmas at all, precisely because of the pagan associations of the December festival.

I would suggest that they are mistaken, that Christmas is not in any significant sense a pagan festival, and that comparisons between Christmas and Hallowe'en are clearly misleading.

## The question of intent

Dating Christmas at 25 December does not constitute an attempt to honour the precise, historic day of Jesus Christ's birth. In fact the day and month were a matter of great speculation in the earliest centuries of Christian history; Clement of Alexandria, for example, writing in the first century, considered that Jesus was born on 20 May.

The first mention of 25 December as the celebration of the nativity comes in 336 AD in Rome; there are no recorded Christmas feasts before the fourth century. At first the Feast of Epiphany (6 January) was the more important festival and was often linked closely with observing Christmas, but by the sixth century 25 December was accepted as Christmas Day (though some branches of the Christian Church still celebrate Christmas on 6 January). The adoption of the December date by the Roman Church was obviously intended to provide a Christian alternative to the pagan feast *Natus Solis Invicta*, renaming the festival of the Unconquered Sun to that of the Son of Righteousness. Originally the new festival was a liturgical celebration, and some of the church controversies of later centuries over the incarnation probably arose because the new festival of Christmas focused attention on the subject.

In the early church there is little evidence to be found that the Christians took over the existing pagan celebrations and simply renamed them. The Christian nativity celebration was a *worship* service. Its timing was not, of course, an accident; it was perfectly logical and necessary for the young church to provide an alternative to the pagan festivals that its converts had celebrated for so long and upon which they had now turned their backs. They had believed that the gods needed to be placated or persuaded; that the worship of the gods was a time of great civic pomp, the highlight of the corporate community year. Now they believed in a dying God, in Jesus whose death had occurred recently and shamefully, in the most humiliating way a person could die, by execution as a common criminal on the Roman's barbaric instrument of justice, the cross; and that having died, he rose again.

These new converts needed to be reminded that their new faith was not in a god who needed to be placated. The ancient sacrifice system of the Jewish people had now found its fulfilment. The king had come to his temple, the stone that the builder rejected had become the cornerstone of the whole edifice. If in the eyes of the world the Conqueror had been ridiculous, the Messiah a failure, the promised Redeemer a freakish galilean prophet riding into town on a donkey—was not this a Saviour who made himself known by changing people's hearts with his new law of love, not by commanding obedience and rewarding it by wild and ceaseless orgies of celebration?

So the church instituted its own celebration: not of a powerful deity but of a helpless baby; not of a genial president of the feast but of one who had come to the world in the person of a human being, the Creator made part of his creation, fully God, fully man, wrapped in swaddling cloths and lying in a manger.

Later, matters became more complicated. For example in Britain, in Victorian times particularly, Christmas became recognisably the modern celebration we know today. Through Victoria's consort Prince Albert, German and other continental practices became part of the British Christmas (the German tradition was linked to the Celtic), notably the element of feasting. The influence of writers such as Charles Dickens was also strong: his *A Christmas Carol* contains all the elements of what today is considered to be a traditional Christmas:

At last the dinner was all done, the cloth was cleared, the hearth swept, and the fire made up. The compound in the jug being tasted, and considered perfect, apples and oranges were put upon the table, and a shovel-full of chestnuts on the fire. Then all the Cratchit family drew round the hearth, in what Bob Cratchit called a circle, meaning half a one; and at Bob Cratchit's elbow stood the family display of glass. Two tumblers, and a custard-cup without a handle.

These held the hot stuff from the jug, however, as well as golden goblets would have done; and Bob served it out with beaming looks, while the chestnuts on the fire spluttered and cracked noisily. Then Bob proposed:

'A Merry Christmas to us all, my dears. God bless us!'

Which all the family re-echoed.

'God bless us every one!' said Tiny Tim, the last of all.[6]

It might almost be said that Dickens, with his wonderfully romantic evocation of the moral power of a sincerely-held Christmas piety, gave an almost religious authority to the glass of punch, the roaring fire, the chestnuts and the remains of the turkey. Though none of these things matter in terms of the central significance of Christmas, they have a huge place in the popular celebration. In the same way the Christmas tree, decorations, cards and garlands became familiar Christmas trappings.

On the other hand, it should be remembered that other decorations from specifically Christian tradition became familiar: cherubs with silver trumpets, Christmas bells, the Christmas robin (associated in legend with the blood of Christ, but included also because, like the holly bush, it flourished in the middle of winter).

But none of these things were what Christmas was *about*. Take them away and the festival lost none of its meaning. Nor did the additions or accretions add anything at all to the significance of the festival. Nobody who seriously considers the meaning of Christmas includes in it any concept of Saturnalia, of cursed mistletoe boughs, or any of the other meanings associated with the symbols. They are dead images, as significant in contemporary thinking as the names of the days of the week: for each of the days (in the English language) bears the name of a pagan deity: the Sun's day, the Moon's day, Tyr's day, Woden's day, Thor's day, Frigg's day, Saturn's day. But the names have no meaning. No possible contemporary observance of any of the days of the week carries with it any sense of relating to the worship or even the existence of those gods. The names of the days are as remote from their roots as Guy Fawkes's night is: for what child, constructing a guy and watching it disintegrate in the flames, has any notion of playing at burning people alive? The point is emphasised by the near-disappearance of the term 'Guy Fawkes' night' and its replacement by the more generalised 'Bonfire night' or 'Fireworks night'.

There is no *intent*, in celebrating Christmas, to include homage to pagan deities. Nor is there any major intent to mark the solar year's turning, the winter solstice; the festival was placed there to counteract the influence of pagan observances that did intend to mark those points. But it would make no difference to the Christian festival if it were to be moved to the middle of August or, as Clement of Alexandria suggested, 20 May (the irrelevance of the trappings of tradition can easily be seen when one considers how Christians celebrate Christmas in Australia, where the turkey can be enjoyed on a sun-soaked beach as readily as in an English winter living room with the heat turned up high against the frost outside). The essence of Christmas remains unobscured by its pagan trappings: it is the festival of the birth of Christ.

Christmas has been compared to the Queen of England's 'official birthday', an arbitrarily chosen date that marks the fact, though not the time, of the anniversary. It's not a bad comparison. In Holland, Christmas and St Nicholas' Eve (6 December) are both observed as festivals, which allows the commercialism and the deeper significance to be separated to some degree. In both cases, there are rituals and ceremonies and irrelevant activities that for many people are a most important part of the event. But the significance of the anniversary remains the same.

### Hallowe'en—a comparable case?

When we turn to consider Hallowe'en, we are looking at something quite different. Where Christmas is a festival to celebrate a single historic event, the exact calendar date of which is essentially unimportant and around which has accumulated a good deal of paraphernalia that carries with it no meaning in terms of the festival's central significance, Hallowe'en's paraphernalia all directly relate to the core significance of the festival.

The pagan origins of the Christmas tree, the holly boughs and the mistletoe would be incomparably more significant if there were significant numbers of people taking part in Saturnalias and worshipping the ancient Roman and Scandinavian gods. But this is not the case. If there are groups of Tigg and Baldr worshippers, or assemblies of people gathering on 25 December to observe the festival of the Unconquerable Sun or the birth of the mystery god, Mithras, then they are so small as to be unknown. If, in celebrating Christmas, we are accidentally celebrating a pagan festival, it is a pagan festival that has long since died and has no relevance or worshippers of its own in modern times. Logically, if this is considered to be a problem, we should also find different names for the days of the week.

But Hallowe'en is different. The trappings from the past that surround the modern festival belong to pagan traditions that are very much alive today. For a number of large and growing religious groups, Hallowe'en is not a dead festival at all. It is, for some, the most important night of the year, far exceeding in importance other festivals, sacred or secular. Membership of these groups is growing. Earlier I mentioned the three organisations of witches. The orders of Druids are even more numerous. There are nine Druidic orders currently active in Britain, for all of whom Hallowe'en is a sacred festival of some significance. The largest, the Ancient Order of Druids, was described in 1991 as having 3,000 members.[7] Another group with a vested interest in Hallowe'en is the growing number of witches and pagans. The 1989 Occult Census recorded a figure of 250,000 throughout the United Kingdom, a figure which David Burnett considers to be exaggerated and suggests a lower figure of no more than 100,000.[8] A third group is those actively worshipping Satan, though these are fewer than is sometimes believed. Burnett points out that practising satanists were the lowest percentage of those responding to the 1989 Census, an observation confirmed by the estimate in the *UK Christian Handbook 1992* that in 1990 there were 180 active satanists in the United Kingdom (30 more than in 1985), organised into two groups both based in England. These figures may seem so small as to be insignificant. However, if accurate, they would make the number of Druids comparable to those of the Associated Presbyterians in Scotland, and the number of witches and pagans in the United Kingdom comparable to the number of believers of the Jewish faith in England.

For such groups, the secular view of Hallowe'en simply will not do. For them the festival is much more than a pleasant exercise of the imagination, playing with spine-tingling but ultimately meaningless fantasies of the occult, against the backdrop of a devil who doesn't really exist and a supernatural that is a handy stockpile of stimulating images and very little more. Uniquely among popular western seasonal festivals, Hallowe'en is virtually devoid of Christian content. It is a celebration that celebrates no central concept of the biblical faith. For the post-Christian West, Hallowe'en represents a night off from the prevailing Christian (post-Christian) consensus.

The trappings, in the public mind, are as remote and ancient as the yule log and the misteltoe. The smiling pumpkin face, for example—who knows or cares that it comes from a tradition of faces carved on vegetables and hung outside the door, as a message to evil spirits that the household was sympathetic to Satan and should therefore be left unmolested on Hallowe'en? A similar inverted passover is implied in trick'n'treat, with its memories of placating the walking souls of the dead. The witch's broomstick and pointed hat have phallic origins—but how many other modern symbols have similar origins! And the masks that decorate the shops at Hallowe'en, the pots of imitation gore, the luminous paint; does it matter that they reflect the masks worn at ancient satanic rituals?

For many, it does not matter at all. It is a trivial piece of fun, and any associations that come with them can be bundled into the dustbin on November 1st along with all the bits and pieces of modern Hallowe'en fun; just as the Christmas decorations end up in the dustbin or in the drawer for next year's fun.

But it is not trivial for everybody. For some groups, the Hallowe'en toys are in fact sympbols of occult power and instruments of pagan worship, charged with meaning, and more so on Hallowe'en. The witch's broomstick is not a child's spooky toy but a symbol of sexual and spiritual energy, the pumpkin mask an image of a reality.

It is all far more significant than any Christmas decoration. It is much more than decorations or trimmings, as we shall see.

## CHAPTER FOUR

# WITCHCRAFT

The bearded young man on television looked normal in every way—perhaps the set was lit rather more dramatically than usual, and he was posed in a slightly menacing way, but it was still a surprise when he announced that he was a witch. He was talking about British Rail's plans for the Channel Tunnel rail link; the proposed route threatened an old lady's house and the site of an ancient burial ground. Six witches of his coven and two hundred members of the public had gathered to enact rituals and cast spells to thwart the route, and the plan had duly been abandoned.[1]

He described the procedure calmly, as calmly as he might have described a protest meeting at the local Town Hall. He said that an increasing number of people were coming to the witches for help, in matters ranging from lost animals to more serious crises. He said that witchcraft deserved to be recognised for what it was; a movement to do good to people, to protect and honour the natural world. There wasn't a broomstick to be seen.

A cynic might have asked whether the people whose houses were demolished to make way for the alternative route had inferior witches or were suffering because they had omitted to consult any witches at all. A political activist might have asked whether public policy ought to be decided by rituals enacted at midnight by minority interests (though somebody who was both cynic and politician might have made some remarks about all-night sittings in the House of Commons in that connection). But it would be hard to fault the transparent sincerity of the young witch, who did seem genuinely outraged on behalf of the elderly and the environment as well as anxious to promote the credentials of his craft.

There is no doubt that witchcraft in the West currently has a much higher profile than it has had for many years. This is partly due to the extraordinary appetite that modern media have for the strange and unfamiliar—television programmes such as *Kilroy, Oprah Winfrey, Donahue* and others regularly discuss the New Age, supernatural and occult in a neutral way and invite leading spokespersons to argue the case for their particular beliefs; daytime chat shows often treat all issues as trivial and religion no more special than any other.

An audience-participation morning TV discussion about Hallowe'en a few years ago, for example, brought together a group of participants including practising occultists, entertainers, nominal Christians, devout Christians, and counsellors of various kinds; the studio was decorated with witches' hats, pumpkins and various other spooky images, and the discussion managed to avoid exploring the issues to any great depth. The distinguished author Ann Pilling, who has written several children's horror stories from an evangelical Christian perspective, was barely given time to speak, let alone raise issues for sensible discussion.[2] The general impression given was that the whole subject was a joke, that any problems people might find in Hallowe'en were not worth discussing seriously, that passionately-held beliefs were good TV (if a vehement argument developed) but that it was not really worth giving air-time to a considered discussion of the issues.

Hallowe'en 1992 was marked by the BBC with *Ghostwatch*[3], a very effective spoof in which TV presenters Sarah Greene, Michael Parkinson and Craig Charles purported to be conducting a scientific, throroughly-documented study of 'the most haunted house in Britain'. Broadcast on Hallowe'en, it showed Sarah Greene and a camera crew spending the night in the house, reporting back on a telephone link to an increasingly worried Michael Parkinson in the studio. As the night proceeded, vaguely worrying incidents escalated into an apocalyptic disaster; as the programme developed, various authentically-portrayed experts argued about the reality of Hallowe'en and occult phenomena generally. It was brilliantly plausible and hugely successful.

The programme was designed to please neither the pro-Hallowe'en nor the anti-Hallowe'en lobby. It made some effective criticisms of media credulity and pricked some bubbles of pomposity in its portrayal of the experts; it also forced the audience to re-examine some of its own attitudes.

What was striking, however, was the accompanying article in the *Radio Times*, where once again the issue of witches was trivialised and gently ridiculed by Sue Arnold as she announced the programme:

> This will be a treat missed by most witches as they will be far too busy dancing 'sky-clad' as they poetically put it (starkers to you and me) around their various ritualistic bonfires. After this, explains my good friend Fay, a witch for 20 years, they will perform a few more rituals with salt and herbs and then tuck into honey cakes, red wine and ale. Why, she adds, as if she's just thought of a special treat, they might even call up a few spirits from the other side for a chat.[4]

In the article Sue Arnold poked fun at most aspects of the occult: Doris Stokes the medium, haunted houses, witches . . . 'Funny thing about the occult,' she observed genially. 'A lot of people who dabble in it seem to favour cardigans.' She further noted,

> Hallowe'en is an extremely important time in a witch's calendar, Fay says, the veil between the two worlds of the living and the dead being almost transparent on this night, making psychic communication that much easier. 'Gosh,' I reply, spellbound by all this. 'Can I come too?' 'Certainly not,' says Fay. 'You wouldn't take it seriously and witchcraft is a serious business.'

Of course the article was written in the context of the BBC's spoof, and Sue Arnold was presumably invited to write it because she is one of the funniest writers currently in print. There is, too, a long tradition of making fun of witches on Hallowe'en, and it is a tradition that has arisen from Christian strength rather than Christian weakness.

The result of articles such as these, however, is to safely stereotype the popular image of the modern witch, as a harmless crank with a desire to do good by startlingly unorthodox means.

> Witches work to bring about peace and harmony . . . Maxine's forte is angelic magic. If, for instance, I wanted a piece of writing placed in, say, *Time* magazine, Maxine would invoke the help of the angel Raphael, who looks after writers. I make a note of the name in my address book. Well, you never know . . .
>
> It is hard to imagine Maxine making waxen effigies and sticking pins in them. But she does, she really does. Not, of course, to bring about ruin and death. Witches do not kill or harm people . . . she might stop a gossip from spreading malicious rumours by cobbling together a doll-like image of the offender, closing its mouth with a safety pin, and hey presto. 'Does it really work?' I ask. 'Every time,' says Maxine. 'More tea?'

It is all cosy, genial and rather fun. The reality is somewhat different. Sue Arnold does not identify 'Maxine', whom she describes as one of Britain's best-known and most respected witches, but the details of the description closely fit Maxine Sanders, widow of Alex Sanders who founded the world-wide Alexandrian tradition of witchcraft and was responsible for much of the publicity that thrust witchcraft into public view in the 1960s. Maxine Sanders is now spiritual head of the movement. John Parker interviewed her in 1991, when she freely talked about her use of effigies, describing one 'case history' of a young woman who had broken up with a male partner. He

> had become possessive and obsessional, refused to accept the break-up and became violent. She pleaded with Maxine to try to

make him stop. And so, within her magic circle, they had to bind this man—not literally but using an effigy—and put something else into his mind to try to make him become interested in something else and forget the girl.[5]

Predicting that some would accuse her of manipulating the man's will, she countered that she was saving him from himself, that it was clearly for his own good: 'he would probably have ended up in gaol'.

Maxine Sanders appears in many studies of modern witchcraft. She now disowns much of the more bizarre activity of her earlier years, particularly those with Alex Sanders. John Parker found her very regretful of the excesses of many who call themselves witches today, of the many charlatans and profiteers. But the image that Sue Arnold presents, of the mild-mannered lady pouring tea in a Bayswater basement while she chats amiably about using home-made dolls to bring a gossip to book, is too benign by half. Maxine Sanders believes in her own powers and is prepared to use them to achieve power over other people. Though she may claim good and positive motives, her work is much more than endearing fun, a wacky twist to the annual Hallowe'en japes: this is serious business, and deserves to be taken very seriously.

What then is witchcraft, in its modern expression?

It could be argued that the most misleading factor in arriving at an understanding of witchcraft is the publicity that surrounds it. We have already looked at some of the ways in which the media tend to trivialise the subject. Sometimes there is an opposite effect: by sensationalism and vague charges, a proper asessment is again made difficult. Headlines such as 'White Witch Bambi Was Locked in a Coven of Evil'; 'Town Fears Satan Rites Cult'; and 'Children Sexually Abused in Satanic rituals, Says Group',[6] tend to stereotype in another way, so that witches are assumed to be—if they exist—all monsters and satanists. Indeed, if satanic abuse is taking place in Britain as I write, it would seem that Satan with characteristic perverseness has used the glare of publicity to cover his tracks brilliantly.

It is not only witchcraft that has come under the media spotlight; all aspects of the occult are considered to be of absorbing interest, and it is a comparatively recent development. In the early 1970s, I was working in Widnes Public Library in Lancashire. Under the national Subject Specialisation Scheme by which every library in Britain was allocated a group of topics and obliged to buy everything published on those subjects—thus ensuring that every book published was bought by at least one British library—we purchased everything published on the subjects of railways, crystallography, spiritualism and sex. Most of the books on the last two subjects were kept in a small box-room away from the public shelves, and could only be consulted by filling in a special form and presenting it at the counter.

The average high-street bookshop today has a more comprehensive collection on both subjects than we had in our entire stock, and the books are freely available for anybody to buy and read.

But in between the popular treatments and the sensational exposés are a number of serious studies of occult themes, often by those who consider themselves neutral observers. Among them are some thorough studies of modern witchcraft. Those who have researched the subject in contrast to the general public image of 'the occult', present a picture of a multi-faceted movement or movements, composed of a number of strands, not particularly averse to publicity and with a level of secrecy comparable to the Freemasons. In other words, the majority of rituals are not protected, though some are jealously guarded secrets known only to those who have progressed in the craft.

David Burnett has identified four streams in contemporary neo-paganism: Wicca, or practitioners of the craft of witchcraft; Pagans, who follow the pre-Christian European traditions; and Magicians. The fourth stream is Satanism, which stands separate from the others because of its explicitly anti-Christian position. Within the Wicca (witchcraft proper), Burnett identifies three paths: the Gardnerian, the Alexandrian, and the Dianic.

The Gardnerian path originates in a key event in the development of modern witchcraft, the publication in 1954 of Gerald Gardner's *Witchcraft Today*. Its publication was only possible because the witchcraft law had been repealed in 1951. Today when witchcraft is hardly news any more, it is strange to think that less than forty years ago it was illegal to be a practising witch; the repeal ended centuries of attempts to stamp witchcraft out by law, during which time many women who were not witches died, many more were persecuted, and certainly many who *were* witches were executed.

For much of the twentieth century, witchcraft was regarded as superstition, an intriguing residue of the past; when Montague Summers, a clergyman scholar with an extensive knowledge of occult literature, published his major work, it received a predictable response:

> His *History of Witchcraft and Demonology* (1926) caused amazement not so much by its content as by the fact that here, in the twentieth century, was a scholar who apparently believed quite simply in things which the generality of educated persons had for some two centuries dismissed as superstition.[7]

Such a response is hard to imagine today, but in 1954 witchcraft was still considered to be a relic of a dark and foolish past. But Gardner's book demonstrated to the general public that the long, largely oral tradition of witchcraft had survived the centuries. A strange book—much of which has been rejected by various modern witches as derivative and gullible—it had an effect on witchcraft similar to the publication of such books as Walton Hannah's *Darkness Visible* on Freemasonry.[8] On one hand it offended those witches who realised that Gardner was revealing hidden secrets of the craft; on the other, it made witchcraft less bizarre and to that extent more acceptable to the public. It also drew considerable public attention on to all matters to do with witches and on to

Gardner himself. One Hallowe'en, the national press arrived in force at a wood in Hertfordshire where he was known to hold coven meetings, the nudist colony who also used the wood providing a convenient distraction away from what was actually going on. As it happened Gardner's witches were not there on that occasion, but the publicity forced him to move elsewhere.

Alexandrian witchcraft originates with Alex Sanders who claimed to have been initiated into witchcraft at the age of seven in 1933, in a bizarre ritual. As a wealthy adult (people gave him large sums of money on the briefest of acquaintances, spellbound—possibly literally—by his charismatic personality), he early learned how to make use of publicity as a cloak for his activities. He seems to have repudiated an earlier interest in Black Magic to devote himself to the wicca craft, and he established links with Gardner, who gave him copies of some of his rituals.

The publicity surrounding Alexandrian witchcraft squandered much of the public interest following the 1951 legalisation, and by the 1970s it was clear that if witchcraft was to have any public credibility at all it needed to present a more acceptable face. It was at this time, John Parker suggests, that the term 'white witch' became widely used—not only to make a distinction against Satanism but also to emphasise to the public that witchcraft could be good and positive—even wholesome and religious. It was a major, and necessary, public relations exercise.

The third of Burnett's 'wiccan paths', the Dianic, draws its beliefs from theories that witchcraft is an ancient cult of Diana taking its inspiration from ancient Mediterranean religions.[9]

My reason for setting out this information is to make some distinctions and clarify some terms. A witch of the wiccan path is not the same as a satanist. Many witches would repudiate the conventional stereotypes of witchcraft. The present enormous surge of witchcraft's popularity dates from circa 1951, and within witchcraft there are several traditions.

The various beliefs of witchcraft are often unformalised,

and few wicca paths have an organised theology. Some common beliefs, have been summarised by David Burnett as follows:

1. The Earth goddess
2. Polytheism
3. The transpersonal nature of the human psyche.

Burnett emphasises, however, that the concept of a systematic theology is alien to wicca beliefs.[10] This also tends to be the case with the New Age Movement, with which wicca shares a belief in the goddess. From this belief comes strands of feminism, earth reverence, nature spiritism, and other characteristic wicca teachings. Intrinsic to the concept of the goddess is the presence of a complementary male god, and wiccan polytheism has produced much discussion about the figure of 'the horned god' who has been a major element in occult writings—not always with the specifically satanic implications the title would suggest.

The third of Burnett's characteristics, the psyche, is too complex for full discussion here, but it is important to observe the relative moral structures of witchcraft, the emphasis on self-fulfilment through the craft, and the high value placed on personal freedom. Good and evil, guilt and sin are not familiar concepts in witchcraft. Instead a view of positive and negative energies is commonly held, which must be kept in balance; a 'white' witch may sometimes act in a 'black' manner to preserve the cosmic balance. This does not necessarily mean that witches are depraved or even more sinful than any other fallen human beings, but it does certainly mean that at the crucial interface between humanity and godhood, witchcraft and Christianity have very little common ground. There can only be an uneasy sharing of some basic understandings of the dignity of human beings and the preciousness of the cosmos. In theological and indeed pastoral terms, wicca and Christianity are doomed to be perpetually at war.

## CHAPTER FIVE

# SATANISM

A parish church, in a commuter village in the home counties. It's a village church, not very old as village churches go, but it's built near a site which has great significance for a wide range of pagan and New Age groups: a convergence of ley-lines, ancient landmarks believed to connect centres of cosmic power and distribute the energy throughout the landscape. Pilgrims come to the old church nearby, now almost a ruin, and meditate and pray there. Whether or not it's because of these associations of power, there have been a few strange happenings at the new church. Traces of what seem like animal sacrifice have been found there. The doors, normally kept locked in case of vandalism, have sometimes been damaged. The altar cross was found to have been interfered with on one occasion and the ashes of a fire found blowing round the churchyard.

In some churches, such incidents increase dramatically at Hallowe'en.

\* \* \*

It is fair to say that as one discovers more about witchcraft, and about Druidism which we discussed in earlier chapters, the festival of Hallowe'en—at least in its modern guise—loses a little of its legendary reputation for horror, mayhem and evil. Many of the stereotypes of Hallowe'en simply do not apply to modern practice. Some who have denounced the festival have denounced it for practices which most witches and Druids would denounce too. This does not mean that Hallowe'en is no longer a problem; it is. But it is sensible to make distinctions and avoid treating what is a multi-faceted phenomenon as if it were a single unified one.

At the same time, it would be foolish and optimistic to pretend that witchcraft and Christianity can co-exist as if both were fellow-seekers after a similar truth merely with somewhat different concerns and emphases. The concepts that lie at the heart of witchcraft and of Druidism are mutually exclusive with Christianity. Even at the simplest level, Druidism's willingness to collaborate with a wide range of religions is a problem to any religious faith that holds to distinctives: for example, American druidism claims links with Hassidic Judaism. While any dialogue and friendship between Jews and Christians is something that all should welcome, it would be stupid to pretend that either Judaism or Christianity would be prepared to let go its central interpretation of the status of Jesus Christ for the sake of religious harmony. If Druidism can conceive of a religious fellowship operating at the deepest religious levels of the human heart, which can ignore such differences, it is hard to see how either a devout Jew or a devout Christian could see Druidism as an ally.

The testimony of witches to the role of spirits and super-natural guides in the previous chapter also raises insuperable problems to anybody who proposes to take the Bible as in any way normative for faith and conduct, for, as we shall see later, the Bible clearly forbids several practices that for wicca are definitive. I would not wish to give the impression to any reader that a desire to see Christian courtesy, dialogue and proper evaluation of religious movements with which Christians do not agree, should in any way lead to a minimising of the gulf that exists between the beliefs in question, whether the witches be black or white and the druids be ancient or modern.

Nevertheless, there are categories within witchcraft; and, as we have seen, witches are not an amorphous undistinguishable mass. A significant sector of modern paganism embraces many things that other parts of the movement reject. Satanism, or shaitanism, is a minority (though in the opinion of some experts, a fast-growing one) within pre-Christian religions in contemporary Western society. And for satanists, Hallowe'en is a great focus of the year, the night when the doors into the spirit world are open wide. On that night many practices and rituals, which according to Druids and witches are long-abandoned and forgotten, are honoured and observed in satanic circles.

## Do what you will

Satanism, which as we have already seen has been estimated to represent four percent of the neo-pagan movement, is a church which worships the devil. In modern times several notorious individuals have contributed to a resurgence in organised satanism.

### Aleister Crowley (1875–1947)

Crowley's influence on modern occultism is profound, and his rituals (usually depraved and obscene, and derived from sexual energy) are still respected by many practitioners. He was brought up by parents who were members of the Plymouth Brethren, but he showed early signs of sadism and cruelty, expressed for example in brutality to animals. He became sexually promiscuous in his early teens. During his career he took for himself the apocalyptic titles of 666, the Master Theiron, and the Great Beast of Tottenham Court Road, and adopted the much-quoted and ambiguous slogan, 'Do what thou wilt is the whole of the law. Love is the law, love under will.'

When he came of age he inherited a fortune, which enabled him to indulge his ambitions to explore depravity and various occult movements. He was revered by his followers, but others were scandalised by his activities, and rumours of black masses and blood sacrifices terrified his neighbours. He was involved in many international occult societies, some of which continue today, and wrote extensively.

His notoriety turned to public disgrace when, in a miscalculation reminiscent of Oscar Wilde's, he sued a former friend for libel after she accused him of practising black magic in her autobiography. His own statements at the trial appalled the public, and he spent his last years as a recluse in Hastings, though maintaining his influence in occult circles. For his public funeral in 1947 he composed a Black Mass, which included a prayer to Satan.

Many modern satanists deny much of his reputation, but it was a self-created one, for he wrote freely of his views. He was also the friend or acquaintance of a range of celebrated writers and public figures—though often they came to disown him—and their accounts of his statements and actions are also available.

I mentioned earlier my time in the 1970s as a member of staff of Widnes Public Library—a typical public department with pleasant, dedicated staff and certainly no brief to promote occultism. By an accident of the national subject specialisation scheme for libraries, Widnes was obliged to acquire Crowley's writings. They were kept away from the public shelves, and the Library Authority dealt with their publically-owned collection of bizarre esoterica as responsibly as they could; periodically the volumes were posted to readers in various parts of the country who had applied to borrow them. They also appeared in the Widnes Central Library catalogue, and local borrowers (who, after all, had paid for them with their rates) could request them.[1]

I was on duty when two young men returned several volumes of Crowley with a request that the books never be loaned to anybody again. They told me they had been trying out some of Crowley's rituals and had had some terrifying results. I could not discover exactly what had happened, but they were extremely shaken young men. It is the kind of story, I know, that is seized on and ridiculed by Crowley's defenders, for no proof of anything was offered; but if the story proves anything at all, it proves that Crowley's influence can still disturb, long after he wrote his books.

*Anton LaVey (b.1930)*

On the night of the Spring Equinox, 1966, Anton LaVey inaugurated his Church of Satan and announced the beginning of the reign of Satan.

LaVey, whose background includes Romanian and Russian ancestors, was introduced to occult lore by his grandmother, a Romanian gypsy. A student of occult and satanist writings from his early years, his explicitly atheistic beliefs draw on a number of traditions which have been well discussed by John Parker and will not be repeated here. His Church of Satan (its headquarters a black-painted building in San Francisco) is the largest organisation of its kind; actively recruiting and publicising, it is one of the strongest centres of satanic prosyletising. LaVey, like Alex Sanders, is a master publicist, using the modern media's insatiable appetite for the bizarre to promote his satanist gospel. The Church of Satan inverts Christianity in a blasphemous mockery of its tenets, practices, rituals and conventions. The intent is less to promote Satan worship than to attack the Christian Church.

John Parker[2] lists the 'nine satanic statements' which LaVey proposes as the equivalent of the Ten Commandments:

1) Satan represents indulgence instead of abstinence!
2) Satan represents vital existence instead of spiritual pipe dreams!
3) Satan represents undefiled wisdom, instead of hypocritical self-deceit!
4) Satan represents kindness to those who deserve it instead of love wasted on ingrates!
5) Satan represents vengeance instead of turning the other cheek!
6) Satan represents responsibility to the responsible instead of concern for the psychic vampires!
7) Satan represents man as just another animal, sometimes better, more often worse than those that walk on all

fours . . . who because of his divine spiritual and intellectual development has become the most vicious animal of all!

8) Satan represents all of the so-called sins as they all lead to physical, mental or emotional gratification!

9) Satan has been the best friend the Church has ever had, as he has kept it in business.

These statements are taken from LaVey's *Satanic Bible*, a compendium of blasphemy and insults to Christianity. Satanism considers vengeance to be one of the highest qualities, and a good deal of its vengeance is directed at the Christian church (for example, the satanic movement has announced a Decade of Vengeance to counter the Evangelicals' announcement of a Decade of Evangelism).

## The deeper cruelty

It's an indication of the rapid growth of interest in satanism and Black Magic that one can with little difficulty obtain plentiful information about groups such as the Church of Satan and individuals like Crowley, LaVey and others. It would be extremely easy to quote much more offensive material, and to do so would in a sense be helping those who originated it.

But it's worth bearing in mind that several people mentioned in this book, and a great many more besides, have skilfully used publicity and public scandal in at least two very deliberate ways: to promote the cause, as a means of effective advertising; and, often, to camouflage what is really going on. To multiply examples of satanic blasphemy and obscenity would perhaps serve both purposes too.

There are two other reasons why I have not chosen to load this chapter with appalling quotations. The first is that a minority of satanists would not subscribe to the gross and obscene practices that have been reported in recent years, any more than to the symbolic, atheistic 'satanism' of LaVey. The second is that the obscenity of satanism can sometimes be much more comprehensive and pervasive than Black

Masses and sacrificing cockerels on the bodies of naked women might imply.

There is one photograph in John Parker's book which is more horrific than any of the numerous explicit verbal descriptions of bestiality, abuse, violence, blasphemy and other outrage that he provides. It is a photograph of Anton LaVey, standing in front of an 'altar' which is a naked woman lying on a leopard skin; he is holding a sword with which he is saluting a young child dressed in a hooded gown and medallion, perched on the leopardskin with the naked woman. According to the caption, LaVey is calling on 'the Prince of Darkness, Ruler of this World', to observe the child's initiation into his Church of Satan. The child is his three-year old daughter, Zeena.

A publicity photograph obtained through a commercial agency, it raises a huge number of questions. Even if the photograph is a posed spoof, a young child was involved; if it was a fake (and parts of the photograph as reproduced in the book look slightly suspicious) there is something extremely distasteful in using images of young children in this way, especially one's own child. If, as seems at least possible, the initiation did take place, one can only speculate about what further experiences the child might have gone on to have. But even to initiate a child into an organisation that includes among its basic tenets such values as vengeance being preferable to forgiveness, is peculiarly horrible. Mental and spiritual cruelty, as child protection agencies are well aware, can have even deeper and longer-lasting effects than physical or sexual cruelty, perhaps, the more so, paradoxically, as LaVey's 'commitment' to Satan is a means to his anti-Christian end rather than a genuine satanic belief.

What we are witnessing in the photograph, as in so much of the Church of Satan's publicity and practice, is quite simply an abomination.

### Satan's new clothes

The increasing public profile of both witches and Druids in recent years has radically altered public perceptions of both;

most people who have come into contact with either, or have even seen them represented on television, would concede that the old stereotypes no longer apply in the majority of cases.

This change of public image has happened for several reasons: the growing acceptability of pagan faiths in Western post-Christian society; the evident sincerity of many for whom these are far from trivial activities; some extremely effective public relations, and in some cases a willingness to allow the public some access to the rituals, ceremonies and claimed benefits. Many members of mainstream religions, while profoundly disagreeing with the beliefs and practices of witchcraft and Druidism, would accept that paganism should be treated like any other religion with which they disagree.

Satanism is different. What revelations there have been from practising Satanists, and certainly what modern satanists themselves have written, confirm rather than contradict the ancient stereotypes. The hackneyed images of devilry from old Hammer horror films turn out to be fairly near the truth. Because blasphemy and inversion of Christianity is central to Satanism, the black candles, desecrated altars, hideous masks and distortions of Christian elements all have a place. Even if, like the Witch King Alex Sanders, modern satanists are creating a smoke-screen of deliberately grotesque and bizarre public activities in order to distract the public from a hidden real agenda, there are enough accessible outlets for serious satanic literature and resources to indicate that much of satanism is as our culture has imagined it.[3] Which is not to be wondered at: several of those who have helped to shape modern popular images of satanism—for example the novelist Dennis Wheatley —are known to have had a serious interest in the subject and to have researched quite deeply into it. Not all satanists are involved in blood sacrifices, desecration, and the like; but many appear to be.

## Ritual abuse

Of all aspects of satanism that have caught popular interest and concern, the wave of reports and allegations of satanic abuse of children is probably the most powerful. It became a major news story in the late 1980s in the wake of the Cleveland child abuse scandal, and reached a high point in the Orkney abuse case. Along the way were reports of children who had been subjected to gross indecency, girls deliberately made pregnant in order that their babies could be used for sacrifice, children brought up in satanic circles and initiated into satanism at birth, and reports of actual child sacrifice.

It is not appropriate, in a section of a chapter in a short book, to embark on a detailed investigation of the satanic abuse scandal. But I want to say four things.

First, in among the press hysteria and the conflicting statements from a range of interest groups, one fact appears to be proven; that there exists a variety of child abuse, usually sexual abuse, in which the abusers make use of the para- phernalia of satanism as the props and accessories of their crime. Thus children report strange rituals, costumes, bizarre settings, sometimes sacrifice of animals. The NSPCC, who have consistently argued that children should in the main be assumed to be telling the truth, have at the same time been cautious in using the term 'satanic abuse', preferring 'ritual abuse' as a more accurate description. The Society remains agnostic as to whether the abusers are believing satanists; it is certain, however, that ritual abuse has taken place.

Secondly, to disbelieve every account of satanic abuse, in the sense of practicising satanists using children in satanic ceremonies and usually with appalling consequences for the children, commits one to disbelieving the testimony not only of children but of an increasing number of adults. It is becoming increasingly unlikely that every such person is either a liar or a mentally disturbed individual. For many, their stories have been told in the context of Christian testimony. To reject their accounts would be inconsistent with the ready acceptance that is given to many of all faiths and none who testify to profound spiritual experiences without 'hard evidence' to prove what they say; the accounts of the freed Iran hostages would be just one example. The problem with modern scepticism is that it is much more disposed to believe a good spiritual experience than a bad one, and to tolerate accounts of a God it does not believe in much more than accounts of a devil it does not believe in either.

Thirdly, an increasing number of researchers have come to the conclusion that there is a core of truth in allegations of satanic child abuse. John Parker quotes with approval the opinion of Canon Dominic Walker of Brighton:

> Ritualized abuse was undoubtedly a fact of life. He was equally certain that some cases were satanic in origin; but to say that it was widespread, to encourage the belief that the world was in the grip of a satanic conspiracy, laced with horrendous practices, was merely to slip into the jargon of the excitable Christian activists and the born-again brigade.[4]

Another investigator who has alleged murder and abuse of young people was Tim Tate, whose book *Children for the Devil* was published by Methuen in 1991 to widespread publicity. Another journalist, Andrew Boyd, produced a book *Blasphemous Rumours*[5] on the subject in 1992 and followed it up with a television investigation; his work was based on the firm conclusion, having examined reports and other evidence from people claiming to be witnesses and victims, that satanic abuse was happening and on a significant scale. It would now be possible, if one were to discount the allegations of evangelical Christians and others whose stories have been widely ridiculed in the media,[6] to find cause for considerable concern in other apparently more sober accounts such as the three mentioned above.

Fourthly, in the nature of the case there is little actual evidence that *could* be produced. Much of what has been presented has been proved to be false, which simply means that a proportion of the claims made are false, which one would expect statistically in any case. But what would constitute 'evidence' for satanic abuse? The problem with the search for evidence is that it often presupposes what evidence it will find. Much of the discussion in print about satanic and ritual abuse begins with the assumption that there is no such thing as Satan and that there can therefore be no such thing as satanism.

One immediate response to this (and it is one that has been made, for example, by the NSPCC) is that satanism does not require Satan. Many religious movements in history have been founded on beliefs that have been proved to be quite mistaken; the quite complex theology of certain primitive tribes trying to make sense of modern aeroplanes is just one example. Other religious movements have been founded by people who cynically created a myth and a creed and sold it to their followers knowing it to be false. That is why the NSPCC, as we have seen, remains agnostic on the question of *satanic abuse*, but uses the term *ritual abuse* freely: even if Satan does not exist, they believe, the evidence of children questioned by NSPCC officers suggests that some people calling themselves satanists (either because they believe he does exist, or because he is a convenient excuse for their desire to abuse children) are subjecting children to abuse that follows the patterns traditionally associated with satanism, devil-worship and the Black Mass.[7] The concern goes back several years; for example, the following statement was made in 1989:

> It seems clear that children are being sexually abused, threatened, coerced, frightened, and physically assaulted in ritualistic cere-monies. A major fear must now be that children have been killed or that the lives of others are seriously at risk . . . The NSPCC is very concerned that children must be listened to and that profes-sionals and parents should not simply discount children's testimony as fantasy.[8]

The NSPCC position of agnosticism is a fair one, and it permits meaningful action to be taken in a situation where there are few familiar guideposts. And it appears very likely from the published reports that there *is* a major problem in Britain of individuals with no real interest in Satanism but with an appetite to use satanic ritual as an excuse for abusing children. But the NSPCC's constructive agnosticism is different to the position taken by a large sector of the population and reflected in a cross-section of 'experts': where agnosticism turns into conviction, not that the devil exists but that he does not.

It is part of an anti-supernaturalism that is very widespread in our modern culture. Take, for example, the controversial book published in 1983 entitled *The Holy Blood and the Holy Grail*[9] in which three authors announced and interpreted what has become known as the 'mystery of Rennes-le-Chateau'. Their theory was that Jesus married, fathered children, and was given drugs while on the cross that enabled him to survive. His family, they argue, eventually settled in France where the bloodline of Jesus merged with the great royal dynasties of Europe. They argued further that a secret society exists that is still active in France and possesses some kind of incontrovertible proof which they may well decide to present to the world in due course.

The book is a fascinating example of academic double-vision. In the first half, which deals with mediaeval and other sources, the authors' method is acceptable. They avoid pre-judging, they are sceptical even about sources they think might help their case, and they take great care to consider whether there might be more than one conclusion to be drawn from the evidence. They also show an understanding of mediaeval thought and the conventions of mediaeval literature. When they turn to the Bible, however, they change their method completely. They ignore the theological dimension (for example they are suspicious that Jesus is said to have died quickly, but the Bible clearly states that he gave up his own life) and there is a distinct anti-supernatural approach employed: assuming that miracles and the like are impossible, they look for other explanations as the only credible ones.[10]

A similar anti-supernaturalism can be seen in many discussions of ritual or satanic abuse. It is taken for granted that there could not possibly be any group worshipping a personal devil and carrying out abuse and murder of children because they believe that to do so will please Satan and gain influence and power. Any cases that look convincing must be cases of adults *pretending* to be satanists, dressing up as an excuse to abuse children.

Of course there is a strong likelihood that such individuals exist—but why not the other kind? The Indian government has outlawed blood sacrifices in the Kali religion: but Edith Schaeffer tells the story of a young man who arrived at L'Abri Fellowship in Switzerland having escaped from a group of Kali worshippers. He had been looking forward to a great ceremonial sacrifice of initiation, and had discovered that he was to be the sacrificial victim.[11] In various parts of the world evidence of human sacrifice is accepted by anthropologists, and is considered real enough in India to warrant a government ban. What is so special about Britain and America that such practices might not be happening here?

It must be strongly emphasised again that satanists represent a minority of the modern neo-pagan movement, though the size of that minority and its rate of growth remain unknown, and that blood sacrifice, if it exists, is almost certainly a small minority within that small minority. There is hysteria in this field as in many others.

It's interesting, however, to speculate what would be the implications of assuming that 'the devil' does exist; that a totally evil entity, with personality, is active in the world and seeking to influence and control people so that they serve the cause of darkness rather than light, of cruelty rather than kindness, of revenge rather than forgiveness.

Some obvious strategies would be open to such an entity—let's call him the devil. Superstition would be his biggest ally. Generations of credulity, the scandal of women through the ages drowned or burned at the stake for having deformed nipples or a practical skill with folk medicine, the examples of Salem, Louvain and many more would all serve his cause; when so many have gone wrong, how can any of it be true?

Public ridicule would be another ally. Cases such as that where a child claimed that scars on her abdomen were from a ritual ceremony, only to be proved wrong by the surgeon who identified his own appendectomy stitching, would suit his purposes very well. Clear cases of wrongful removal of children by social workers, preferably in the middle of the night, would be very helpful too.

And, it must be said, a level of hysteria among Christian activists would help the devil's cause too. Use of emotive language, attempts to compensate for lack of hard evidence by weight of rhetoric, importing flamboyant experts from overseas whose manner with professionals is unfortunately patronising—all very helpful. One cannot doubt the sincerity of the woman counsellor who, challenged on television to produce evidence of satanic abuse, could not do so and could only reiterate her conviction that satanic abuse was taking place: but for many viewers it must have been convincing evidence that the devil does not exist.

Such statements might reinforce the theory that as 'left-hand' rituals do not require actual abuse to take place—it is enough that the victim believe he or she is being abused, so that the ritualist can tap the psychic energy of the victim's fear—some accounts of ritual abuse by witnesses 'and survivors' might be accounted for by drugs and suggestion, hence the lack of evidence. Yet this by no means proves that the devil does not exist.

If he does exist, as Christians (and others too) have traditionally believed, then the underlying anti-supernaturalism in much of the media has provided a most effective smokescreen over his activities. But the media portrayals themselves are complex; as we shall see in the next chapter.

## CHAPTER SIX

# HALLOWE'EN IN THE MEDIA

As Hallowe'en has become increasingly popular in modern society, and the entertainment and commercial aspects have become more established, Hallowe'en has taken a much more prominent place in the media. In this chapter we will look at some examples.

## Television and cinema

Hallowe'en is often the cue for a television carnival of horror extravaganza. It would be strange if it were not so, for television's business is to reflect the culture in which it operates, and Hallowe'en is an important annual event in Western culture.

In America, for example, where it is celebrated by many adults as well as children, an episode of the television comedy *Roseanne* was set in the middle of Hallowe'en celebrations: Roseanne was sulking and refusing to go to the Hallowe'en party. In a pastiche of Charles Dickens' *A Christmas Carol*, she was visited by a succession of ghostly guides: Hallowe'en Past, Hallowe'en Present and Hallowe'en Future. They helped her in an entertaining process of self-realisation that followed Dickens closely. The episode was very funny, and very well written. Shown as it was on British television too, it must have made many British viewers realise that Hallowe'en in Britain is still a much smaller business than it is in America.

Hallowe'en often turns up as a minor theme in films: in the thriller *The Little Girl Who Lives Down the Lane*, the horrific sequence of events begins on Hallowe'en night, with children trick'n'treating. It also often appears as an element of other entertainment. The computer game *Superfrog*, one section of which is set in a ghostly castle, uses the maddeningly catchy tune that dominates the film *Halloween Three*, which is discussed below.

But the festival itself is often celebrated in its own right by the arts and media. In 1992, for example, BBC2 television celebrated Hallowe'en with *The Vault of Horror*, 'an all-night Hallowe'en celebration of being scared witless'.[1] Five films were shown, ranging from classic spooky comedy to stronger stuff: 'A rare screening of *Death Line*, a 1972 tale of cannibalism on the London Underground, is a special bonus scare for commuters.' In between, a panel of horror film directors and horror writers discussed the whole phenomenon of horror entertainment. I have already discussed BBC1's contribution, *Ghostwatch*. Channel Four on the same night screened the thriller *The Fog*, and an animated spoof *Vampires in Havana*. There were similar features on Radio 4. *Radio Times* quoted Mary Lambert, who directed the film of Stephen King's macabre and frightening novel *Pet Semetary*:

> In order to live with your fears, you have to face them. That's the purpose served by scary movies and scary stories, the same purpose that myths used to serve. If you examine your worst nightmares, you'll find that they're funny. Mine are, anyway.

It's an argument that has some validity, and has been very well expressed by Stephen King himself in the introduction to his volume of short stories, *Night Shift*:

> When you read horror, you don't really believe what you read. You don't believe in vampires, werewolves, trucks that suddenly start up and drive themselves. The horrors that we all do believe in are of the sort that Dostoyevsky and Albee and MacDonald write about: hate, alienation, growing lovelessly old, tottering out into a hostile world on the unsteady legs of adolescence . . . The

horror-story writer is not so different from the Welsh sin-eater, who was supposed to take upon himself the sins of the dear departed by partaking of the dear departed's food. The tale of monstrosity and terror is a basket loosely packed with phobias; when the writer passes by, you take one of his imaginary horrors out of the basket and put one of your real ones in—at least for a time.[2]

This characteristic of horror literature, the 'cathartic' function, is often noted. And it should also be said that horror literature and horror films do not exist in isolation. They are part of a complex cultural representation of modern society, reflecting a wide range of pressures and concerns; a role well illustrated by the following comment by an Australian writer on the media:

> The violent protagonists of *A Clockwork Orange*—in contrast to the staid, withdrawn, and opulently self-regarding victims—were emphatically young and they moved about in a psychedelic world which at times had the appearance of a global disco . . . The young men in this film were as worrying in their violation of traditional social and ethical norms as was the blaspheming and horrifically transformed teenage girl in *The Exorcist*.[3]

Underlying much sociological critique of horror, however, is the same assumption that we saw in the previous chapter; that the occult has no reality, that there is no supernatural evil active in the universe, that the issue is not so much whether a spiritual danger exists but whether behavioural, social or other human problems might or might not be caused by the genre. A further point is that made particularly by the libertarian lobby against censorship, who argue that much that is commonly regarded as obscene, blasphemous or excessively violent actually performs a useful function for society and to censor it would be a costly mistake.[4]

These arguments are serious ones, but we shall not study them in depth here. The argument that surfaces much more frequently at Hallowe'en is the argument for the annual jape; a holiday devoted to horror films and occult publications, on the basis that as they are all meaningless fantasies anyway, there is no reason in the world—except possibly the proviso that 'It's all a bit childish really'—not to have fun with them. It is that argument we will be considering as we look at a few typical Hallowe'en offerings.

## Hammer Horror Films

It would be an unusual Hallowe'en if television were to screen no films made by the Hammer House of Horror, a British company that operated after the war from an old house near the Thames which appeared as the setting for a long list of lurid films. Hammer made versions of the Frankenstein and Dracula films, with innumerable sequels; they made many other films too, almost all with a supernatural flavour. Stars such as Peter Cushing, Christopher Lee and Vincent Price dominated the cast lists.

The earliest Hammer films tended to be in the genre of morality fables, their occult and satanist content being, in the main, graphic illustrations to a fairly conventional version of the traditional good-versus-evil struggle. Dr Frankenstein and a range of his descendants created a succession of monsters, all of which went wrong; Dracula was repeatedly vanquished only to rise again. But there was a genuine pathos underlying the Frankenstein films, and the Dracula legend never (in Hammer's hands) presents evil as triumphant; however many times Dracula rises from the grave, there is always a Christian symbol that will defeat him. For many, including myself, this is too reminiscent of right-through-might magic and shamanism to be an entirely comfortable Christian myth; but though the theology of the early Hammer productions is a faint pastiche of the biblical gospel of the risen Christ, it does at least concur with that theology insofar as it touches the eternal verities at all. (It would be naive in the extreme, of course, to think that Hammer films at any stage of the company's existence were motivated by anything but entertainment and box-office success.)

The decline in Hammer films was rapid, as the company

succumbed to the demands of an increasingly gory and thrill-seeking horror market, and as censorship of films relaxed allowing the women characters to reveal more and more of their bodies, and sex and eroticism to be more openly portrayed on film (a number of later Hammer films ventured into portrayal of lesbianism). But there was a more fundamental change. The functional good/evil morality of the early films began to give way to what amounted, in the emphasis on believable and horrific portrayal of horror, to an invitation to celebrate evil. In the earliest Hammer epics, the enjoyment of evil had been cloaked in a suitably explicit condemnation of it.

It's a change that has sometimes been regretted by the stars themselves. It is interesting that Peter Cushing has the reputation for being a man of strong moral views who has shunned the Hollywood lifestyle to which his career entitled him; and Vincent Price, in a newspaper interview made some years ago, deplored the decline of the old films, remarking that whereas once the theme was the overcoming of evil by good, today films glorify evil.[5]

Some Christians, and believers in other faiths, would urge that all horror films be shunned, on the grounds that imaginative involvement with evil can only be bad.

It's a position one can sympathise with and it is certainly easy to apply. It should be added, however, that to be consistent one would have to make the same decision about detective stories and quite a lot of contemporary cinema and television that might not immediately seem to be comparable. Some do make that decision, and rule most entertainment out of their lives.

On the other hand, it's possible to chart a course through these difficult waters, and detective stories are a useful analogy. A novel that invites its readers to glory in the murder, that regales its readers with graphic descriptions of the killing, the state of the corpse, and similar aspects of the plot, is one thing. A novel that invites the reader to join in the search for the killer, to exercise one's brain in examining clues and to admire the skills of the detective in successfully concluding the investigation, is another. Even so, some will reject Sherlock Holmes as unsuitable reading, and some will read enthusiastically authors whom I would want to reject. But the analogy does reflect that in this area and that of horror films, like so many other areas of modern arts and media, categorisation is not only possible but essential. With the changing standards of Hammer and other films of the genre, there is plenty of scope for defining, and applying, criteria.

Some films, however, are single-minded in their emphasis and are encumbered by hardly any residual post-Christian morality at all.

## Halloween (the film)

As an occasion, Hallowe'en is not something we British set much store by, but to Americans it has been a source of childlike wonderment and terror that has inspired numerous stories and films. This latest vehicle for the talents of John Carpenter is a good old fashioned clutching hand melodrama with a few psychological overtones and a fashionable line in mild eroticism.[6]

This 1978 film is set in a small American suburb on Hallowe'en night, but has very little supernatural content. A well-made, thoroughly unpleasant shocker, it concerns a rampage of killing on Hallowe'en by an escapee from an asylum who goes back to his home where, at the age of six, he murdered his older sister when he found her having sex with her boyfriend. He proceeds to terrorise two homes where the parents are away from home, having left teenage babysitters in charge of their children. It was one of the earliest films in a genre that depicts teenagers (often sexually adventurous ones) at the mercy of marauding, motiveless evil—*Friday 13th* being another classic of this kind; like *Halloween*, its monster wears a mask, and like *Halloween* it has spawned a series of poor-quality sequels.

At the end of the film, the monster appears to have been destroyed, but his body is found to have disappeared without trace, leaving only a faint impression in the ground. This leaves a rather clumsy suggestion that the killer may have been a supernatural visitation given human shape. But there are many loose ends.

It's a strange film, hard to categorise. In a sense it is a portrayal of the age-old, Hammer-style battle between good and evil, for the evil is clearly condemned and though the ending is inconclusive there is no suggestion that evil has actually *won* in any absolute sense. The supernatural element is left very vague; there is not much suggestion that the Hallowe'en activities have raised up a demon or in some other way caused the catastrophes of the night. The killer is also shown to be exacting some kind of moral retribution in revenge for his sister's immorality; it is the promiscuous babysitters who come off worst.

On the other hand, the film transparently intends to entertain not by the spectacle of evil being defeated but by wallowing in evil's violence. It offers an orgy of violence, and places it in the vaguest of moral contexts. The 'mild eroticism' is especially disturbing as it revolves around extreme violence directed at young teenagers.

All of which may seem to be making very heavy weather out of something intended as mere entertainment. 'I went, I saw, I was suitably chilled,' said the reviewer. 'What more could one ask of a Hallowe'en treat?'

Perhaps in 1978, when Hallowe'en was still a minor festival and crazed serial killers had not achieved the notoriety they have today, it was all one might have asked (though hopefully it would still have been worth questioning the moral value of entertainment that drew heavily on violence, voyeurism and terrorising of children). In the mid-1990s, many will have major reservations.

## Halloween Two

Carpenter's 1981 sequel was an excuse for a further orgy of violence as the murderer from the previous film escaped from the asylum again, fifteen years later. This time the havoc takes place in a hospital, which gives ample opportunities for scalpel-slashing and other graphic special effects. Donald Pleasance repeated his role of the agitated psychiatrist from *Halloween*, and the film ends with the murderer apparently incinerated in a hospital fire.

## Halloween Three: Season of the Witch

For the 1983 sequel Carpenter handed direction and writing to Tommy Lee Wallace, who worked on a screenplay written by British science-fiction writer Nigel Kneale (who later asked for his name to be removed from the credits). It was a departure from its predecessors, using none of the characters or storyline, but placed much greater emphasis upon the supernatural element of Hallowe'en.

The story features Conal Cochran, a toy manufacturer who is marketing a range of Hallowe'en masks. Advertisements for his product dominate all the television channels as the festival approaches. There will be a wonderful Hallowe'en treat for all children who are wearing his masks, he promises, if they tune into his commercial (which they are to do straight after the film *Halloween* has been screened on nation-wide TV). But Cochran is an inveterate (and, it transpires, extremely perverse) practical joker; Hallowe'en night is to see his biggest joke yet. He has stolen one of the Stonehenge standing stones, and chips of it have been implanted in every mask sold; by using an arsenal of modern scientific techniques harnessed to the power of ancient Celtic ritual, he plans to massacre thousands if not millions of children when they tune in for the big surprise.

The film is a combination of a lurid science-fiction/horror thriller and a poorly made detective film (as the hero and heroine set out to discover what's going on), with special effects that are particularly violent and frightening. Film reviewers, many of whom regard *Halloween* as a classic of its kind, have been dismissive of *Halloween Three*:

> *Assault on Precinct 13* and *Halloween* prove Carpenter's creative strengths; shambles like *Halloween II* and *III* demonstrate weaknesses better left undisplayed.[7]

Students of film may well criticise me for ignoring several levels of creativity, social significance and contained meanings, on all of which levels the *Halloween* films function. But this is not a book of film criticism and I want to make a single point about *Halloween Three*: that it cannot be treated purely as entertainment. Its theme is child abuse on a colossal scale; the use of occult powers for evil ends; the potential for evil to conquer the world.

These are not abstract ideas dreamed up by a versatile storyteller. They are ideas that are on many agendas in today's world.

Perhaps the films have a function in reminding us that human beings are capable of evil (though the television news is doing the job perfectly well already). Perhaps they have a cathartic function, in that those who watch them in a sense purge their own capability for evil and become in some way better people as a result. Perhaps the literary and mythic quality of the films removes them from the kind of moral criteria we would apply to other areas of human life (though that would require more enthusiasm for Carpenter's achievement than most critics seem willing to show).

But one thing is certain. Stephen King's argument, that horror deals with imaginary fears, does not apply here. The fears in the *Halloween* films are metaphors for real fears.

And of course in some films, the metaphor ceases to be a metaphor at all and becomes the thing itself.

## Rosemary's Baby

This film, directed and written by controversial director Roman Polanski, was made in 1968 and is a cult favourite for the Hallowe'en season. Polanski (born in 1933 in Paris, of Polish parents) had already established a reputation for portraying violence, cruelty and psychological terror in a number of successful films—including *Knife in the Water, Repulsion*, and *Cul-de-Sac*.

In *Rosemary's Baby* a young couple move into an apartment where they initially find the attentions of their elderly neighbours, an old-fashioned couple with some odd ideas, rather irritating. But gradually the husband becomes intrigued by them and begins to fall under their influence, displaying disturbing behaviour patterns. The couple have just decided to start a family and the wife thinks she is already pregnant; now she has a horrific dream, which culminates in her being led naked by her husband and their neighbours into the neighbours' apartment where, in a strange room surrounded by shadowy observers, she is ritually raped by a figure who is clearly the devil. As she shrieks in pain she screams out her sudden realisation: 'This is no dream!'

As the pregnancy develops the couple's behaviour becomes increasingly strange and the neighbours increasingly possessive. Eventually the film concludes with the birth of the child. The neighbours—by now clearly seen to be satanists—are in full control of the situation and the birth is greeted by the attending coven with delight; the last moments of the film are an extended paean of praise to Satan.

The film, for which actress Ruth Gordon won an Oscar and for which Roman Polanski (as writer) was nominated for one, has become a cult classic and is seen as a precursor of *The Exorcist* and other films.

As Hallowe'en fare, is there much difference between watching this and watching one of the old Hammer horror films? A great deal of difference. First, the film is an authentic satanist tract. It relies on inversion of Christianity throughout, and its greatest inversion is at the end; it was the first film to be understood to be celebrating not the traditional triumph of good over evil, but evil rampantly triumphant. The content of the film is the same as that contained in many published statements by satanists. This alone should cause Christians (and many believers in other faiths) to be appalled by it.

Secondly, Polanski's own life would indicate that for him the issues of the film were more than mere entertainment. Polanski's wife, film star Sharon Tate, and several of his friends were members of the group surrounding the notorious Charles Manson, who taught a mixture of sex, drugs and occultism. The year after *Rosemary's Baby* was released, Sharon Tate and other Manson followers were dead, in a bloody slaughter that horrified the world. Manson's links with satanism are well known.

Thirdly, and most disturbing, the film received the full blessing of the satanist movement. A well-known satanist was invited to advise on the making of the film to ensure authenticity. His name was Anton LaVey, the founder of the worldwide Church of Satan which I have already discussed. And the actor who plays the part of the devil in the film is Anton LaVey.

## Books

The theme of Hallowe'en has always interested writers, and of course it has had a special fascination for writers interested in the occult and supernatural. For many older writers, however, the festival was merely a part of an interesting tradition. Montague James, the Provost of Eton College and celebrated writer of ghost stories, did not make much of Hallowe'en in his fiction and, to judge from his letters, paid little attention to it in real life. In a letter of 1935, written on 27 October, the Feast of Saints Simon and Jude on the following day occupies his mind but Hallowe'en is not mentioned.[8]

As Hallowe'en has become a more prominent festival, however, its treatment in literature and the place of the books themselves has changed. Bookshops and libraries frequently arrange Hallowe'en displays and other promotions of horror titles, and the theme is an increasingly popular one in children's literature and school activities. One writer of adult fiction whose books are sure to be prominent in Hallowe'en book productions is Dennis Wheatley.

### Dennis Wheatley (1897–1977)

Wheatley was a well-connected wine merchant, having entered the family business on being invalided out of the Navy in 1919.

In 1932, struggling in the face of the recession, he sold the business. He became a full-time writer and his books were soon million-sellers.

A major theme in his more than fifty thrillers was black magic and the occult, in the reality of which which he clearly deeply believed; Hallowe'en and Walpurgis Night are landmarks in his occult thriller plots. He claimed that he himself had no practical experience of the subject, but his research was extensive and thorough. He knew several leading experts on the occult (including Montague Summers), and travelled the world in search of new information and colourful material for his books. Early editions of his novels carry a warning:

> I desire to state that I, personally, have never assisted at, or participated in, any ceremony connected with Magic—Black or White.
>
> . . . I have spared no pains to secure accuracy of detail from existing accounts when describing magical rites or formulas for protection against evil, and these have been verified in conversation with certain persons, sought out for that purpose who are actual practitioners of the Art . . . I found ample evidence that Black Magic is still practised in London, and other cities, at the present day.
>
> Should any of my readers incline to a serious study of the subject, and thus come into contact with a man or woman of Power, I feel that it is only right to warn them, most strongly, to refrain from being drawn into the practice of the Secret Art in any way. My own observations have led me to an absolute conviction that to do so would bring them into dangers of a very real and concrete nature.[9]

Some modern satanists are exasperated by what they consider to be Wheatley's unhelpful focus on all that is most sensational in satanism; on the other hand, his books show a familiarity with the literature of Black Magic, and as he himself pointed out there is a large amount of material available. His work for this reason serves as a summary of published satanism, doubtless over-credulous and dependent upon secondary sources but nevertheless showing the fruit of his wide research.

The disclaimer quoted above is hard to take seriously. Apart from anything else, it is a very effective advertisement for the books: what better commendation than that the author had met and talked with Black Magicians and had an extensive knowledge of his subject? And in 1935, if he *had* announced himself as a practising satanist, Wheatley would have been in trouble with the police, so the disclaimer is dubious on those grounds too. However, it is unlikely that Wheatley *was* a practising satanist, for the connection would by now have been exploited both by satanism's friends and satanism's enemies.

As a warning it is even less effective. The whole selling power of Wheatley's occult novels lies in his detailed descriptions of Black Magic and satanism. Like many million-selling popular novelists, he has a mastery of plot and very little else; his characters are poor and their conversation is stilted. If Wheatley had seriously wished to deter his readers from involvement in the occult he would have written very few horror stories and contented himself with his adventure and crime stories, which would have secured him fame and fortune. But he built a world-wide reputation on occult fiction, saw several of his novels filmed, and became extremely rich. Through his writings many people first became interested in the occult.[10] For this, whether or not he believed his own disclaimer, Wheatley was responsible.

When you curl up with a Dennis Wheatley novel for a spine-tingling Hallowe'en read, you are not reading fantasy. In whole or in part, there is a reality behind what he writes about.

### Charles Williams (1886–1945)

As prolific a writer as Dennis Wheatley (writing an average of two books every year during the last fifteen years of his life), Charles Williams was a Christian with wide scholarly interests. He was a friend of C.S. Lewis and a member of the close Oxford literary circle known as the Inklings, where Lewis, Tolkien, Williams and others met to share their manuscripts, read scholarly papers, and debate theological and other issues. Williams, who was an Anglo-Catholic Christian, had been involved in a Rosicrucian secret society when young, but later disowned it.

Among Williams' large literary output is a series of seven 'supernatural thrillers', ranging from the first of the series to be published, an adventure story called *War in Heaven*, to the complex and arcane *Shadows of Ecstacy*. The last, published in the year of Williams' death, is entitled *All Hallows' Eve*;[11] it is one of the few novels in which the heroine is dead when the story begins.

Lester Furnival only gradually realises the fact that she is dead. London is deserted, the only other person to be seen—apart from a last, fleeting sight of her husband—is a sad waif-like woman called Evelyn who was killed in the same accident as herself; together they embark on the afterlife. Among the living, the evil Father Simon—dedicated to the pursuit of power through magic and witchcraft—is seeking to achieve the ultimate power, that over life and death; he wants to be lord of the dead and be worshipped among them. But Father Simon's power is not infinite, and the barriers between the living and the dead work both ways. Just as evil extends from the living Father Simon to attempt to ensnare the newly dead Lester and Evelyn, so Lester's love extends back; and repentance and forgiveness become major themes of the novel. Behind the central episodes of the novel stands the cross, both implicitly and in allusions that are characteristic of Williams' writing; as in the description of Father Simon ('The Clerk'):

> His servants had, at his will, attempted his death and he had foiled them. But so doing, he had refused all possibilities in death. He would not go to it, as that other child of a Jewish girl had done. That other had refused safeguard and miracle; he had refused the achievement of security. He had gone into death—and the Clerk supposed it his failure—as the rest of mankind go—ignorant and in pain. The Clerk had set himself to decline pain and ignorance. So that now he had not any capacities but those he could himself gain.[12]

So in a novel that is not afraid to explore the supernatural implications of Hallowe'en, Charles Williams proposes against sorcery and evil a greater power: the power of the Christian gospel of the crucified and risen Christ. It is what C.S. Lewis would call a deeper magic. Like Wheatley's writing, this is not fantasy: and just as thousands of pagans would confirm the reality underlying Wheatley's writing, so thousands of Christians would confirm the truths that Williams was underscoring.

### Ann Pilling (b.1944)

Ann Pilling, winner of the 1986 Guardian Award for Children's Fiction, writes from an evangelical Christian perspective, though much of her fiction has been published by secular imprints. Notable in her earlier work are four horror novels for children: *Black Harvest, The Beggar's Curse, The Witch of Lagg*, and *The Pit*. Of the first, nominated by school-children to be included in a 1984 British book promotion, one young reader said: 'It was like opening the door of a fridge.'

*The Beggar's Curse* follows the pattern of all four. The author has often said that her proviso, when accepting her publisher's invitation to write horror stories in the first place, was that she would write about real horrors, not imaginary ones; that there exist aspects of life that deserve to be viewed with horror and pity, as much by children as by adults. So her stories concern the Irish potato famine, the power of ancient evil, the persecution of Scottish Covenanters and the tragic death roll of the Great Plague of London. But in each book, too, there is a symbol of redemption, a pointer to a larger dimension in which perspective the dramas are played out. In *The Pit*, for example, the fantasy horror of the boy's magazines and fantasy games are compared to the spectacle of death as death, the exposed ancient skeletons in the accidentally opened plague pit. For the boy, it is a growth into understanding.

*The Beggar's Curse* is a novel about a village shadowed by darkness, where flowers do not bloom and birds do not sing.

The annual Easter play appears very sinister to the three children who arrive in the village for their holidays.

> 'It doesn't sound very Christian to me,' she said suddenly.
> 'Oh well, it's not dear, anything but. All the religious bits have been stuck on, over the years. It's not really supposed to be done at Easter, either . . .'[13]

In a postscript, Ann Pilling explains that the village play is based on her childhood memories of Hallowe'en mumming plays in Cheshire and her experiences of 'soul-caking'. The play, which centres around a horse's skull, was a relic of ancient pre-Christian horse worship.

The story becomes darker when the children learn that the village was once cursed by a mysterious beggar; and in a grisly scene they witness the preparation of the horse's head for the play—a real horse's head, being boiled clean in a smoky shed. More and more disturbing facts emerge about the village's history, and the inhabitants behave in increasingly bizarre ways. Even superstition is warped:

> The buns were called 'Soul Cakes' and the idea was that you ate them to increase your strength. 'Of course, they're supposed to be eaten at Hallowe'en,' she said, 'when the year's dying. Not in spring. You don't need new life in *spring*, for goodness sake. But this village got it wrong as usual.'[14]

The resolution of the oppressive, frightening world of the village and the events that gather horrific speed as the novel comes to its climax bring the two worlds of pagan religion and Christianity into sharp contrast; there is nothing in the novel that comprises a Christian sermon, but the Christian themes of redemption and restoration are pointed out with clarity. When one of the children, Prill, almost dies in hospital, her return to life is described in a sequence of symbols that not only express Christian concepts but are also the opposite of what the children have seen in the village:

> Something was happening to Prill behind the lifeless mask. It was as if she was coming back along a little black road, all on her own

after some great journey. At first it was very quiet, then a bird started cheeping up in a tree, and she heard a soft beating noise which gradually became louder and more distinct, and which she finally recognized as a church clock.[15]

Thus Ann Pilling accompanies her dramatic portrait of horror with an encompassing portrait of good. Even the distortion of Hallowe'en customs being transferred to Easter serves her purpose; though the shadowy rites of the village mummers dominate the novel, resurrection and light are never far away, whether in the festival of Easter itself or in the light that bathes Prill as she is restored to life.

These are only a few examples of the relationship between Hallowe'en and the arts and media; there are many more.

The same question underlies each of the examples I have quoted. In what context do we see Hallowe'en? Is it a glorification of pretend horror, celebrating an evil that docs not exist, whether in order to exorcise our fears or simply to enjoy kicking over the traces of normality for one night of the year? Or is it an opportunity to celebrate violence and evil acts for their own sake, real or imaginary? Is it a night with special significance, because we respect the pre-Christian traditions that have made it a special night, and wish to pay some kind of homage to those traditions? Or is it a night when the powers of darkness enjoy a futile rampage against the greater power of God, their conqueror in a battle that is already won?

Such questions are relevant not only to the formal world of films and books and television, but to imaginative creativity of all kinds. One particular field where Hallowe'en has had an increasing influence is that of fantasy role-playing games. To this subject we turn next.

## CHAPTER SEVEN

# HALLOWE'EN FUN AND GAMES

Welcome, gentle reader. Possess you the skill to avoid prancing death? What shall you do at midnight, when the talon taps? Is the tomb your own? It is in the nature of adventure to question; conversely, questions lead to adventure, as these questions lead to yours. Within these pages you shall quest into darkened chambers and forbidden secrets, and seek out adventure to answer the questions posed. In doing so you shall find yourself *Alone On Halloween*.

*Alone on Halloween: a Solo Scenario Against the Children of the Night*. A scenario for the fantasy roleplaying game *Call of Cthulhu*

(Scenario published 1992, by Pagan Publishing)

### Fantasy role-playing games: the background

Not surprisingly, the debate about Hallowe'en has extended into the hugely popular hobby of fantasy role-playing games, best-known to the general public for the most popular example of the genre, *Dungeons and Dragons*. Based as they are on fantasy worlds peopled by a variety of natural and supernatural denizens, these games lend themselves readily to the Hallowe'en theme (as can be seen from the quotation above).

The multi-million pound phenomenon of fantasy role-playing games has attracted a great deal of debate on its own account, and the major arguments revolve around its alleged fascination and promotion of the occult. Many role-playing games do centre on supernatural rather than military warfare, and it's common to find parents, church leaders and youth organisations campaigning against the industry (players' ages range from around twelve years old and upwards: many play on into retirement, and college students are a particularly active group of hobbyists. The British game company Games Workshop, by contrast, identifies its key market as the middle teens, which reflects a drop in the age of the average target group in recent years[1]). On the other side of the debate is ranged a wide spectrum of educationalists who recognise that the games have often made readers out of children who were totally uninterested in books, youth workers who commend the social interaction that the games (which are played by a small group of co-operating individuals) promote, and games enthusiasts who acknowledge that the fantasy role-play concept is one of the most innovative and stimulating developments in the industry for a very long time.

I would like to examine this debate a little, to put into perspective some of the references to Hallowe'en and the occult that tend to occur more and more frequently over the last few years in fantasy role-playing literature and the games themselves.

It is a debate that has been marked by vagueness and hysteria on both sides. Some objectors have clearly never actually looked at one of these games, for they talk of gameboards, winning the game, and 'scoring'—none of which apply to fantasy roleplaying in anything like the way the critic assumes they do. On the other hand, the hobby press has often given a platform to anybody with a vaguely religious and ethical approach to life, to explain why as a 'practising Christian' or member of another faith they had no problems with playing the games. The hysteria can get out of hand too: stories of fantasy role-players driven to suicide by playing the games almost always turn out to concern people with serious personality disorders whom one might expect to have troubles regardless of their recreational tastes. On the other hand, the now-defunct *Gamesmaster International* magazine once printed a letter from a reader arguing passionately that the Evangelical Alliance, who had publicly criticised role-playing games, were well-known to be behind the Orkney child abuse scandal; one was left marvelling as much at the stupidity of the magazine's legal advisers, as at the Alliance's good-humoured restraint in their letter sent to the magazine, easily refuting the nonsensical allegations. So it might be a good idea to clarify our terms before going further.

First, Christianity is a specific faith which does not have vague generalisations at its core; it is much more than a moral creed or an ethical code. At the heart of Christianity is an infinite God who possesses personality and is capable of communicating and offering salvation to his human creations. Central to the Christian gospel is the principle that God's salvation is achieved by Jesus Christ bearing the sins of mankind through his death on the cross, validated by his miraculous rising from the dead and confirmed by relationship between humanity and God. The necessity for salvation in the first place arises from the fall of mankind from original innocence and the finite but supernatural power of a personal devil.

Secondly (for there is often misunderstanding on this too, not least by many Christians) let me give a definition of fantasy role-playing, taken from one of the hobby's own publications:

> The easiest way to understand a role playing game is to think of it as a work of fiction . . . in a role playing game, the author (called the Gamesmaster) only determines the setting and some of the basic elements of the plot. The actions of the characters (and thus the plot) are determined by the game 'players' and the Gamesmaster . . . Each player assumes the role of (role-plays) his 'player character' and the Gamesmaster role plays the non-player characters. In other words a fantasy role playing game is a 'living' novel where interaction between the actors (characters) creates a constantly evolving plot.[2]

The 'Gamesmaster' is often called the 'Dungeon Master', though some games have their own title for the equivalent task. But in all fantasy role-playing games, there are no winners such as one finds in conventional board games, and the action takes place in the players' imaginations; though imagination is often aided by miniature figures, models and other accessories.

## Are fantasy role-playing games occult resource packs?

A charge often levelled at the games is that they are really packages of resources for the occult. It's easy to see why, when most shops specialising in the hobby carry whole shelves of books bearing titles like *Monster Compendium, The Grimoire, Fiend Folio, Ars Magica, Spell Law*, and many more. But none of these books contain instructions on casting spells or other occult activities; they enable the player to *role-play* doing such things, and what the likely results will be. Thus the game books will not give you a ritual for summoning a demon, but they will provide you with copious information on the probability of the character you are playing being able to do so, and the capabilities and likely disposition of the demon thus summoned. On that score, the hobby has been unfairly criticised, often from scant knowledge or understanding.[3]

But that's not the whole story; for when one examines the games that are being published today there is an authenticity to the atmosphere of the game scenarios when portraying the supernatural that is not accidental. Though many of the fiends, demons and monsters are fictitious and have no basis in fact or in occult lore, they are clearly invented by imaginations that have been educated by extensive reading in the literature of the arcane, the occult and in some cases the satanic. For example, the game *Call of Cthulhu* is based entirely on the work of the novelist H.P. Lovecraft (1890–1937), who invented the 'Cthulhu Mythos', a bleakly macabre literary world: 'For those who like the thoroughly ghastly, the loudly macabre, with all the stenches and moans of ravished churchyards, this is the book,' commented one reviewer.[4]

Players of the game are encouraged to read several of
Lovecraft's books beforehand, and the influence of Lovecraft's
familiarity with arcane and spiritist writings can be seen in the
various supplements and accessories to the game. Similarly,
the *Manual of the Planes*, a supplement to *Advanced Dungeons
and Dragons* offering 'vast new worlds of adventure . . . from
Arcadia to Pandemonium, from the plane of elemental Fire
to the Astral plane . . .' acknowledges inspiration from a
range of sources:

> Though I consulted many texts to gather the mythological and
> theological information in this book, some topics were just not
> addressed in these sources. When faced with the question of what
> Indra's realm looks like, or the nature of the Yggdrasil, or what
> is to be found on each of the Seven Heavens, I employed a time-
> honoured Dungeon Master process. I made it up . . .[5]

While it is only fair to the author to emphasise that much
of the book is a work of imagination, it is worth pointing out
that his research among 'many texts' was to aid his research
into a range of topics that includes the Nine Hells, the Astral
Plane and the Abyss.

Critics of fantasy role-playing games who have jumped to
the conclusion that the rule books and accessory volumes are
little more than occult practitioners' manuals have misunder-
stood how the games work. But the books could be considered
to be something that is, potentially, just as dangerous; com-
pilations of authentic, half-authentic and fictitious documentation prepared against a backdrop of the occult, the arcane and
sometimes the satanic.[6]

In this context, the frequent references to Hallowe'en are
disturbing, for though the festival is rarely taken seriously in
the games, the sources from which information is taken in
order to portray Hallowe'en authentically can often be highly
specific. Thus the 'Halloween Issue' of the magazine *Autoduel
Quarterly*, published for players of a game based on road
violence in the future (and whose editor runs discussions on
how to handle anti-fantasy lobbies) contains an article

on decorating one's car and race-track (battle arena) for Hallowe'en.[7] The author writes with a heavy-handed humour that is typical of much of the *genre*, but the general atmosphere of this 'Halloween Issue' seems to relate to a much wider context which, though probably not subscribed to, is appealed to by implication.

Similarly, a series of scenarios for the game *Dark Conspiracy*, published in the role-playing magazine *Challenge*, are on the theme of 'Dark Hallowe'en'; again, the writer is obviously drawing on the literary tradition of the occult, though it is unlikely that he himself has any faith commitment to it.[8]

## The fighters at the gates of Hell

Fantasy role playing games have traditionally drawn their main moral structure from the age-old theme of good versus evil. Human beings are capable of good, and they are capable of evil; it is better to serve good than to serve evil, and good will ultimately triumph despite any temporary victories that evil might achieve. So the argument goes, and you'll find it in Hans Andersen, *Mother Goose, The Wizard of Oz and The Never Ending Story*—and countless more works of imagination besides.

It's a moral framework that is only to be expected when one considers the earliest influences on fantasy role playing games. Gary Gygax, who is acknowledged as the founder of the genre, devised the first edition of *Dungeons and Dragons* out of his interest in fantasy literature and mediaeval warfare (played with model soldiers on a table-top). The fantasy literature that forms so strong an influence on fantasy role-playing was, and is, profoundly dominated by the work of J.R.R. Tolkien and in particular his epic trilogy *The Lord of the Rings*. Tolkien was a devout Roman Catholic, friend of the popular apologist C.S. Lewis and the novelist and essayist Charles Williams, both of whom were Christians and to both of whom Tolkien read drafts of his work. While all three vigorously denied that they were writing educational allegories of the Christian faith, their work is clearly controlled by and driven by a Christian world view and a very clear biblical concept of salvation.[9]

J. Eric Holmes is an American, a lecturer in neurology who edited the 'Basic Set' of the *Dungeons and Dragons* Rule Book and has been involved in the hobby since 1974 when it began. He readily acknowledges the good/evil framework of *Dungeons and Dragons*, while conceding that the issue does become complicated in the context of a game:

> It is true that most good fantasy stories assume a struggle between good and evil or Law and Chaos, or God and Devil, but these are usually determined by the internal rules of the story. This wider, rather vague, orientation of the D & D universe is hard to understand, but, fortunately, need not have much influence on the playing of the game. I suspect this alignment obscurity may be related to the author's apparent Christian bias [because Yahweh and Jesus are omitted from the game to avoid giving offence] . . . [10]

Holmes was writing in 1981, and the second edition of the rules published in 1990 has much improved the alignment system so that the game operates much more clearly within the struggle of good and evil.

To sum up: mainstream fantasy role playing games involve a group of players cooperating to achieve a common purpose, which can be anything from the survival of the group to the defeating of an evil that threatens the community or even the world. On the way players can gain fame and fortune, but the overall cast of the gameplay is the working out of the traditional role of good: to be other than evil, and eventually to overcome it. The players consequently are recruits in the eternal struggle, battling often at the very gates of Hell to gain victory over the powers of darkness.

In that context fantasy role playing games have some worthwhile points in their favour, though there remain a large number of worrying aspects to the hobby even in its mainstream form that warrant a more informed debate than the one that has been conducted in many quarters so far.[11]

**Taking the Devil's side**

If the fantasy role-playing game industry were operating exclusively in the perspective of good versus evil, the debate would be much simpler, not least in the context of Hallowe'en, where the fragile relationship of good to evil depends on the tacit assumption that good is in fact superior to, and more to be desired than, evil. One would then commend the correctness of the basic moral orientation, draw attention to the possibility of players developing an unhealthy interest in too graphic a portrayal of evil and the occult (an interest easily fed by the present industry, which provides numerous manuals of statistics and details of fictional and pseudo-fictional denizens of the worlds of supernatural evil, sprinkled with a few 'authentic' creations drawn from religious and occult literature), and raise the matter of use of time, obsessive play and one or two similar, related issues. However many reservations might be expressed—and no doubt a large number would be expressed—the commitment to the age-old conflict would secure the fantasy role-playing industry a position well within traditional story-telling.

Unfortunately, in recent years sectors of the fantasy role-playing industry have taken a quite different direction. Where previously it was maintained throughout the hobby that the existence of evil characters in the game (usually 'non-playing characters' controlled by the Gamesmaster) was intended purely to provide symbols of evil to be opposed and defeated by the players, some recent games have allowed players to role-play characters that are by no means dedicated to the cause of good, in whatever way the term might be interpreted.

*Lost Souls (Marquee Press)*

This game, published in America in 1991, is not very well known in Britain, but copies turn up in shops specialising in role-playing games: I purchased a copy in a games shop in one of the larger towns of Surrey. It is typical of a type of game that is becoming popular.

The back cover of the rulebook summarises what the game is about.

### Lost Souls: Adventures in the Afterlife

*Lost Souls* dares to explore undiscovered territory. Starting where other games leave of [*sic*], you enter the afterlife as a spectre striving to collect karma. With daring and wit, you'll be reborn a higher being. But don't lose your Will to Live too soon, or you may come back as pond scum! As a spirit, you'll face unprecedented challenges. Only an ingenious use of your supernatural powers will see you through the post-mortem mayhem of *Lost Souls*! . . . If you enjoy problem solving, role playing, and incredible adventures, then *Lost Souls* was made for you!

### Things to Do When Dead

- Return to haunt your killer
- Help lost souls find peace
- Battle demons on their own terms
- Confront evil spirits in supernatural combat
- Explore bizarre planes of the dead
- Make ghostly vows not to rest until you achieve your personal goals
- Come back as one of 21 ghost types—from an apparition to a wraith![12]

The rulebook is written in a doggedly humorous style ('Dead is dead, and there's no going back to that used-up bag of meat you used to be'.) As with most similar games, players create characters for themselves in order to role-play a game scenario. The rule-book helps in this by providing details of 21 different types of ghost and detailing the special powers and characteristics of mediums, arcane scholars and a range of other types of people from which the player chooses who he or she was before death.

Among the enemies the player may meet in the game (apart from the person who caused their own death) are Crypt Lurkers, Ghouls, and Hitler. The latter is described as an evil spirit, an incorporeal vapour: 'Hitler has retained his overwhelming need for power and attention in death. His hypnotic eyes and stirring rhetoric are so compelling, spirits find themselves obeying his every command . . . Strangely enough, Hitler is kind to children and animals, and treats them well.'

Among powers that players may possess are: Animate the dead, Aura of death, Charnel breath, Exorcism, Hypnotism and Rotting stench.

Among suggestions provided for Gamesmasters to create new game scenarios are the following: 'Demon Wars', 'Madness Takes its Toll', and 'Evil Possession'.

Devotees of this game would probably point out that it is intended to be humorous, and that the occult and super-natural trimmings are provided to dress up what is ultimately an old-fashioned horror story; to take it seriously, it will be argued, is to misunderstand and grossly misjudge what the game is. Players playing the game are unlikely to be taking it very seriously either, and fears of widespread occult celebra-tions using the game as a resource are probably misplaced.

Yet the game represents a disturbing trend on several levels. First, on the level of acceptability; use of Hitler as a trivial character in a recreational game will be distasteful to many people, and the added twist that he treats children and animals well will increase the offence. Secondly, although the game appears to be intended for older teens and even older, there are no apparent restrictions in shops as to who may purchase it, and many people will question the value of material such as this forming the basis of anybody's extended recreation. Thirdly, and most disturbing in my opinion, the game shifts the traditional orientation in the good-versus-evil conflict. The player, in being encouraged to exact super-natural revenge upon those who killed him, and to dabble in other ways in the stock resources of occult, arcane and supernaturally malevolent powers, begins to blur the orienta-tion altogether. There is little in the game to make the player feel conspicuously committed to the cause of good, and a good deal to make him feel that the darker powers are on his side.

Of course the portrayal of the world of the dead as a world in which contact with and influence upon the world of the living is taken for granted, is a very characteristic element of Hallowe'en; the trivialisation of the concept of free passage between the worlds of the dead and the living, and the glorification of the mayhem that ensues without any very clear moral perspective, is typical of the modern view of Hallowe'en.

### Ars Magica (White Wolf)

The matter becomes much more complex and detailed in the materials provided for the award-winning *Ars Magica*,[13] originally published in 1989 as a finely-crafted recreation of the world of mediaeval magic revolving round 'the Covenant', a fortress in which a group of magi—the Order of Hermes—live and study.

The original game was an impressive piece of literary creativity and made some useful observations about mediaeval thought:

> The world in *Ars Magica* is the world the way the mediaeval folk looked at it; it is as magical as they imagined it to be. It is a mythical setting, and poetic justice is part of daily life. Even the common folk deal with the supernatural, but more infrequently than the wizards. Charms and saints' relics protect them from the evil eye, prayers hold at bay the invisible demons that stalk their villages at night, and ancient curses haunt them. Some leave food on boulders to appease the foreign spirits, and then go to church to pray for forgiveness. The world is alive with magical significance . . .[14]

The authors were careful to point out that they were not trying to construct a magical resource kit but to recreate a world of the imagination. Players role-play wizards, free from superstition, 'learned, creative, free from social constraints, and willing to dare the mysteries' that surround them; constantly studying, but periodically venturing forth to research, gather resources, and help those who need their aid.

As *Ars Magica* has developed, however, it has—like many other fantasy games—developed a highly-detailed and vivid interest in the evils it aims to encourage players to oppose.

Currently in its third edition, it includes in its supplements a volume entitled *The Maleficium*, which draws heavily on scholarly and other sources to provide 'a means to integrate diabolism and diabolists into your Saga' and reminds the reader that 'an understanding of diabolism is necessary before it can be properly portrayed in your game'. It is a compendium of information (for example chapter six: 'This chapter presents some examples of evil spirits that you may use in your stories.')[15]

The author states that he is 'anti-satanism, anti-violence, and pro-humanity', and he urges his younger readers to discuss the book with their parents—'Allay any fears . . . let them give advice and warnings based on religious and moral conviction, and, above all, accept their judgement if they do not wish you to own this book. If possible, sound them out before you make the purchase' (p.7). This is laudable, though I am sceptical about how effective the warning is.

Books such as these present a problem for the concerned Christian critic. One can certainly admire the scholarship and creativity of the book, and the research has certainly been to some extent balanced: the Revised Standard Version of the Bible, C.S. Lewis' *The Screwtape Letters* and St Thomas Aquinas are all listed as sources. It would be a mistake, too, to see this game as being a mindless recreation. It is in a different category to *Lost Souls*, for example: the appeal of the game is the recreation of a world, and playing it is a highly literate experience. Nobody would invest in *Ars Magica* (with the various supplements, it's quite expensive) or devote time to playing it, unless they were genuinely interested in mediaeval thought and magic as a body of knowledge. In other words, this is not a frivolous game.

On the other hand a reading of *The Maleficium* shows that the game breaks the good-versus evil structure even more than *Lost Souls* does. The back-cover comments are disturbing:

Your burdensome choice lies between Light or Dark . . . Choose Dark and all the world is your bauble, its every craven satisfaction yours to relish. You are master over all, magical or mundane. And what is the price for this glory? Merely your paltry, intangible soul. Yet, why does the shadow grin? . . . With this reference Storyguides and players may pierce netherworldly deceptions and secrets, bringing about confrontations with the Evil, and mastery of the Dark Arts. You may now become a Magus opposed to the Light and the Order of Hermes itself.

The authors point out that to do so needs caution: 'Enjoy playing a diabolist while it lasts, and accept a vile end as part of the story. *Ars Magica* is a game of storytelling and morals. To pursue the dramatic and just, rampant acquisition of power and wealth should be balanced with Hell's eventual victory' (p.137).

But however much it is wrapped up in a moralising framework, *Ars Magica* is now a game that equips its players to role-play satanic forces and the attacking of the forces of good; as much a turn-round of the conventional morality of role-playing games as the film *Rosemary's Baby* was a reversal of the traditional if nominal Hollywood moral universe. The title of the *Maleficium* gives a clear enough clue:

Roman law had been stern in dealing with sorcery. The word 'maleficium', originally wrongdoing in general, now came to mean malevolent sorcery in particular, and the maleficius or maleficia was presumed to be closely associated with the devil. Sorcery could now be prosecuted not simply as a crime against society but as a heresy and crime against God.[16]

The game is freely available in any specialist, and many high-street, games shops.

Recent role-playing games raise major questions, particularly in relation to the young. The market that the games are aimed at is a predominantly young one. Though it is fair to say that a game such as *Ars Magica* would be played more by older enthusiasts than the middle teens who make up most of the hobby's clientele, enthusiasts of any age are familiar with the games from magazines and browsing in games shops.

In the context of the Hallowe'en debate, the issue is a simple one, and is not greatly different to that in the previous chapter. No game is neutral, and role-playing games are more effective than most in communicating ideas and values. When we look at the values of many current games, we find them often perilously close to an inversion of the traditional morality that has been widely hailed as one of their most considerable social and educational strengths. Add to that the fact that the imaginative environment of many games is close to the bleak arcane world of horror novelists like H.P. Lovecraft, and the value of some games becomes even more questionable. The fact that fantasy role-playing games are the most intriguing, inventive and satisfying games to have been invented for decades does not make the problems of some of them less; and it certainly becomes advisable for any who have the responsibility of nurture of youngsters—parents, teachers, relatives or other—to look closely at what their charges are playing with; not necessarily to censor, but to be aware.

## CHAPTER EIGHT

# WHAT THE BIBLE SAYS

The great majority of the religious and other groups discussed so far in this book would claim to be quite open to Christians involving themselves in their activities. For example Paul Beyerl, teacher and witch in the Tradition of Lothlorien, states:

> My Wiccan church, the Rowan Tree, includes members who are primarily neo-pagan . . . not all of our members fall into this category. We have a substantial portion of those who identify themselves as Christians, even those who work within Christian churches.[1]

Similarly Chief Druid Philip Carr-Gomm remarks that:

> Many Druids are able to combine their Druid practice and understanding with Christianity or with Wicca . . . It is exciting to find that others appreciate this—the Christians who meet each year at the Conference on Christianity and Druidry, the Wiccans who join in Druid ceremonies and workshops or who meet with Druids at the annual Pagan Federation Conference . . .[2]

The same could be said of many other groups. In the 1960s for example, long before the New Age became the fashionable and socially acceptable buzz-word it is today, a friend of mine who had visited the community of Findhorn described his experiences there to me and urged me to investigate too. The New Age that was coming, he told me, matched the Christian dream, and many Christians were finding at Findhorn a new dimension and deepening of their faith. Circumstances never took me to Findhorn, but I was frequently told that as a Christian I would not be threatened, only blest, by what went on there.

One should take care before belittling everything about these movements (the Findhorn community, for example, appears to have been at that time a genuinely caring group— my friend arrived there unannounced on Christmas Eve, and a senior member of the community slept in an outhouse so that my friend could sleep in a warm bed). Nor should one minimise the value of Christians engaging in constructive dialogue, if that dialogue does not involve abandoning important fundamentals in order to have it in the first place.

But the fact is that the Bible allows such interaction only within very narrow limits. If a Christian takes the Scriptures as authoritative, it quickly becomes very clear that almost all pagan values and practices are forbidden. The only way that one can claim to have a foot in both camps is if clear biblical guidelines are regarded as irrelevant. As these guidelines occur throughout the Bible, to be a Christian Druid or a Christian witch means almost nothing, because it would demand a Christianity drained of its essence.

This chapter therefore examines what the Bible says about a number of the issues we have so far discussed in connection with Hallowe'en. It is not a chapter primarily designed to convince you that the Bible is absolute truth and completely trustworthy and authoritative: that is the task of evangelism and apologetics. What follows is an index, a list of quotations, not a sermon.

When we turn to the Bible we find clear teaching on these issues as on so many others. God's word has a great deal to say about the occult, about witchcraft, about communicating with the dead and many more topics that are important in Hallowe'en. And when the Bible speaks about these things, it always speaks in the context of a war. It is a war between a local prince and an absolute ruler; between the 'god of this world', and the Lord God Almighty.

The god of this age has blinded the minds of unbelievers, so that they cannot see the light of the gospel of the glory of Christ, who is the image of God. (2 Cor. 4:4)

As for you, you were dead in your transgressions and sins, in which you used to live when you followed the ways of this world and of the ruler of the kingdom of the air, the spirit who is now at work in those who are disobedient. (Eph. 2:1–2)

It is a war that revolves around the cosmic struggle between God and Satan. And uniquely among wars that are currently being fought, it has already been won convincingly. The death of Jesus Christ by crucifixion is a victory which, according to the Bible, was foretold in the first days of the world when, talking to Satan who had taken over the serpent's body, God said this:

And I will put enmity between you and the woman,
and between your offspring and hers;
he will crush your head
and you will snap at his heel. (Gen. 3:15)[3]

When that victory happened, Paul writes to the church at Colosse, the triumph was total:

And having disarmed the powers and authorities, he made a public spectacle of them, triumphing over them by the cross. Therefore do not let anyone judge you by what you eat or drink, or with regard to a religious festival, a New Moon celebration or a Sabbath day. These are a shadow of the things that were to come; the reality, however, is found in Christ. (Col. 2:15–17)

Nowhere in the Bible is any involvement with the occult, any process of divination, or approach to sources of supernatural power and influence other than the revealed God of the Bible, described as being outside the context and the battleground of this cosmic battle, being waged 'against the spiritual forces of evil in the heavenly realms' (Eph. 6:12). All who look for truth, the Bible teaches, take up a position for or against Truth. And according to the Bible, there is only one way to the God who is Truth.

Jesus answered, 'I am the way and the truth and the life. No-one comes to the Father except through me. If you really knew me, you would know my Father as well. From now on, you do know him and have seen him.' Philip said, 'Lord, show us the Father and that will be enough for us.' Jesus answered: 'Don't you know me, Philip, even after I have been among you such a long time?' (John 14:6–9)

The Bible is full of stories of individuals and nations who, throughout the centuries, have rejected this revelation of God through Jesus Christ, either rejecting the promise made in the old sacrifice system and God's covenants with Abraham, or later rejecting the death and resurrection of Christ to which the sacrifices had looked forward and which was now a historical fact. They followed other gods and idols.

Although it never encourages a preoccupation with the occult and with satanic activity, the Bible says enough about these matters to have generated a large number of commentaries and studies of the biblical view of the occult and related topics. However, the present book is a book about Hallowe'en, not about the occult in general: so we will be looking at what the Bible teaches on a number of issues that lie at the centre of the festival of Hallowe'en.

## Divination

As we have already seen, many of the activities traditionally associated with Hallowe'en are survivals of divination rituals. It was regarded as a period when the doors into the supernatural and occult were especially wide open, and so was a more favourable time than most for attempting to predict the future.

There are two ways in which the word 'divination' can be used.

### Simple prophecy

If we are talking about 'knowledge of the future', of the kind sought in many pagan rituals and especially at times of other-world access like Hallowe'en, there are obviously many instances in the Bible where knowledge of the future is a matter of fact, not condemned in any way. For example Jesus frequently speaks of what is going to happen in the near and far future, though his knowledge is not limitless (Mark 13:32).

But there is an important element to be noticed. *There is no suggestion that a machinery of knowledge-on-demand is operating*, in the way that many magic practices have traditionally been described (once the formula is known, the magic word uttered, the power summoned—then the super-natural must inevitably yield up its secrets . . .) For Jesus, in the days of his humanity, knowledge of the future arose out of a relationship with his heavenly Father.

It's a theme that is common to all forms of future know-ledge that Scripture authenticates. The prophets were able to deliver astonishingly accurate predictions of the future, and it is often only when the results of modern archaeology are scrutinised that we see how precise some of those prophecies were. But it was knowledge made available to them by God, dependent upon their maintaining the relationship with him. Every prophet had to make the basic commitment that they would serve and honour the God through whom the know-ledge of the future came. Every prophet found his knowledge coming to him by means outside his control. By contrast, to discover the initials of your future spouse by tossing apple-peel over your shoulder is to use a quite different methodology, where once the formula is known, the results are—in theory at least—guaranteed. Like the bar of chocolate that appears when the coin is placed in the slot of the dispensing machine: if you know the method, the ritual, the correct procedure, then the knowledge will automatically follow.

The difference between this and biblical prophecy lies in the fact that prophecy is a *passive* activity: which may seem strange when one thinks of the fiery prophets of the Old Testament and the many acts of courage and initiative they displayed. But none of them had to do anything to become a prophet. Indeed, it's extraordinary how many of them became prophets despite their inclinations. Jeremiah thought he was too young to be a prophet, Jonah was simply scared (and a snob), Isaiah was in the Temple, grieving over Uzziah's death, deeply aware of his own unworthiness; all three had to be hauled kicking and struggling into the prophetic role, and the same is true for many more whom God called. When they spoke God's word it was because God had set his mark on them and given them the prophetic task, not because they had become adepts, studied works of divination, learned from a master of the art, or in fact in any way learned the knack of extracting information from God by ritual or secret knowledge.

### Fortune telling

The kind of divination that is more popularly associated with Hallowe'en is much more trivial. Like the ouija board or the tarot pack, Hallowe'en games have gained a higher prominence in recent years. And for many people, such diversions are purely entertainment without much significance.

The biblical view of divination in this sense is unambiguous and forceful. It forbids it. God gave the Israelites strict instructions as they prepared themselves to enter the Promised Land:

> When you enter the land the Lord your God is giving you, do not learn to imitate the detestable ways of the nations there. Let no one be found among you who sacrifices his son or daughter in the fire, who practices divination or sorcery, interprets omens, engages in witchcraft, or casts spells, or who is a medium or spiritist or who consults the dead. Anyone who does these things is detestable to the Lord, and because of these detestable practices the Lord your God will drive out those nations before you. You must be blameless before the Lord your God. The nations you will dispossess listen to those who practise sorcery or divination. But as for you, the Lord your God has not permitted you to do so. (Deut. 18:9–14)

But many years later the Israelites rebelled and did do just that, and the result was just as God had warned them:

They forsook all the commands of the Lord their God and made for themselves two idols cast in the shape of calves, and an Asherah pole. They bowed down to all the starry hosts, and they worshipped Baal. They sacrificed their sons and daughters in the fire. They practised divination and sorcery and sold themselves to do evil in the eyes of the Lord, provoking him to anger. (2 Kings 17:16–17)

In the prophecy of Jeremiah, the warning is again clear:

Yes, this is what the Lord Almighty, the God of Israel, says: 'Do not let the prophets and diviners among you deceive you. Do not listen to the dreams you encourage them to have. They are prophesying lies to you in my name. I have not sent them,' declares the Lord. (Jer. 29:8–9)

In the New Testament, the story is told of a slave girl in Phillipi who had the gift of divination:

Once when we were going to the place of prayer, we were met by a slave girl who had a spirit by which she predicted the future. She earned a great deal of money for her owners by fortune-telling. (Acts 16:16)

By removing the spirit that possessed her (and ruining her gift of divination in the process) the apostle Paul put himself in considerable personal danger and earned a flogging and imprisonment for himself and Silas—an indication of the value (not least the commercial value) placed on divination.

## Witchcraft

Hallowe'en, as we have also seen, is a crucial night of the year for witches, the practitioners of the ancient pagan *wicca*. Witchcraft embraces a number of practices, including enchantment, sorcery and conversation with spirits and pagan deities. There are many references in the Bible to these and similar practices, and in every case the craft of witchcraft is condemned, even when the motives are not necessarily to promote evil (modern witches are anxious to make a careful distinction between white magic and black magic, and most who would call themselves witches would claim to separate themselves both from black magic and satanism).

Many characters in the Bible practised witchcraft and other occult skills in clear defiance of God, and they are condemned explicitly. Here for example is the sorry story of Manasseh, industriously reversing the piety of his father and re-establishing the occult where it had been removed:

> In both courts of the temple of the Lord, he built altars to all the starry hosts. He sacrificed his sons in the fire in the Valley of Ben Hinnom, practised sorcery, divination and witchcraft, and consulted mediums and spiritists. He did much evil in the eyes of the Lord, provoking him to anger. (2 Chron, 33:5,6)

As before, it must be said that this policy of desecration and deliberate offence to Christianity is not one of which all witches would approve, and that many witches are in everyday life unexceptionable people whose neighbours would be be extremely surprised to discover that they were living next door to a witch. But the Bible does not make distinctions between black witchcraft and white, nor does it acknowledge any shades of grey. Witchcraft is forbidden. Sometimes the reference seems to be to malicious magic:

> The acts of the sinful nature are obvious: sexual immorality, impurity and debauchery; idolatry and witchcraft; hatred, discord, jealousy, fits of rage, selfish ambition, dissensions, factions and envy; drunkenness, orgies, and the like. I warn you, as I did before, that those who live like this will not inherit the kingdom of God. (Gal. 5:19–21)

Yet charms, incantations and spells are forbidden too, as for example in the contemptuous words of the prophecy of Isaiah:

> Both of these will overtake you in a moment, on a single day;
> Loss of children and widowhood.
> They will come upon you in full measure,
> in spite of your many sorceries
> and all your potent spells . . .

> Keep on, then, with your magic spells
> and with your many sorceries,
> which you have laboured at since childhood.
> Perhaps you will succeed,
> perhaps you will cause terror.
> All the counsel you have received has only worn you out!
> Let your astrologers come forward,
> those stargazers who make predictions month by month,
> let them save you from what is coming upon you . . .
> They cannot even save themselves
> from the power of the flame.
> Here are no coals to warm anyone;
> here is no fire to sit by.
> That is all they can do for you—
> these you have laboured with
> and trafficked with since childhood. (Isaiah 47:9, 12–15)

The whole Bible teaches clearly and consistently that witch-craft and Christianity cannot co-exist, and that the gospel of Jesus Christ destroys the power and cause of witchcraft.

## Dealings with the dead

Hallowe'en is traditionally the night for remembering the dead and for expecting, and sometimes provoking, contact with them. But this is yet another area where the Bible is unequivocal in its condemnation; we have already seen in several of the passages quoted above that any attempt to consult with the dead is forbidden, most noticeably in the list of forbidden practices given in Deuteronomy 18:10–11, of which the final mention of those who 'consult with the dead' is comprehensive and leaves little room for negotiation.

### The Witch of Endor

The most dramatic example in the Bible of attempted contact with the dead appears in 1 Samuel 28, where Saul, exhausted and frustrated, facing a new and potentially devastating battle strategy from the Philistines, turns to a medium for help.

Saul's continued flouting of God's commands had alienated him from God, who no longer talked to him as he had before. And now, though he knew the Deuteronomy prohibitions, was aware of the absolute ban imposed by God on consulting mediums, and had himself even expelled the mediums and spiritists from the land—now, at the end of his resources, he went to consult a witch. It was a desperate situation; facing his old enemy on the level ground of Jezreel, where his military strengths were worth little, he was terrified at the prospect of defeat.

> He enquired of the Lord, but the Lord did not answer him by dreams or Urim or prophets. Saul then said to his attendants, 'Find me a woman who is a medium, so that I may go and enquire of her.'
> 'There is one in Endor,' they said.
> So Saul disguised himself, putting on other clothes, and at night he and two men went to the woman. 'Consult a spirit for me,' he said, 'and bring up for me the one I name.' (1 Sam. 28:6–8)

Clearly necromancy had survived God's edicts and the purges of the people's leaders. The woman, after her initial suspicion, agreed to Saul's request to bring Samuel back from the dead. It seems from the biblical narrative that whatever her qualifications or occult powers may have been, on this occasion she succeeded; at Saul's request she summoned up 'an old man wearing a robe' whom Saul instantly recognised as Samuel.

Reading the tersely-told story in the Old Testament, what comes over most strongly is the jangling nerves of those involved. The witch feared that she would be put to death for obeying Saul, was terrified when she recognised him, and was even more terrified when her magical skills worked. Saul, already on edge because of the Philistine threat and the silence of God, persisted in his demand only to find that through the solemn figure of the dead Samuel, God delivered his last, fateful condemnation of the rebellious king.

> The Lord will hand over both Israel and you to the Philistines, and tomorrow you and your sons will be with me. The Lord will also hand over the army of Israel to the Philistines. (1 Sam. 28:19)

Faint with hunger, mad with despair and aware that he had committed a catastrophic error, Saul collapsed. The witch offered him food, but it took the combined efforts of her and his soldiers to persuade him to eat. The fattened calf and fresh-baked bread have the air of a macabre feast; it was the eve of Saul's last day alive.

The story is full of implicit condemnation. There is no suggestion that consulting a medium is a wise or permissible act. There is no hint of the dead waiting in some limbo state to impart wisdom to earnest seekers; wherever Samuel has come from, he has been dragged reluctantly and he feels no sympathy for Saul whatsoever. Even the witch, once she has recognised Saul, is horrified at what is happening.

The story reflects the thrust of the whole Bible. Death is a one-way barrier. The Hallowe'en fantasies of the departed returning to eat food set out for them, of spirits roaming the world in an annual night of freedom, to be placated by ritual observances, have little to do with the biblical picture of the supernatural.

If we are to retain the Bible at all, there is no possibility of Christians joining in the rites of any group that honour Hallowe'en as a sacred night. In fact, it is hard to see, when the Bible is so explicit about the central supernatural focuses of Hallowe'en, how a Christian can with integrity even join in the commercialised, trivialised versions of Hallowe'en traditions; while we duck for apples, serious divination is being attempted by practising pagans; while we light pumpkin candles, some are lighting fires for very different reasons.

## CHAPTER NINE

# THE UNPAID BILLS

In his classic work *The Four Major Cults*, the Christian writer
A.A. Hoekema begins with a reference to a well-worn but
still powerful saying:

> You may have heard the expression, 'The cults are the unpaid bills
> of the church.' Though this statement does not tell the whole
> story, there is a great deal of truth in it. Cults have sometimes
> arisen because the established churches have failed to emphasize
> certain important aspects of religious life, or have neglected
> certain techniques. Though one may assign many reasons for the
> rapid growth of the cults, one reason we may be sure of: people
> often find in the cults emphases and practices which they miss in
> the established churches.[1]

It must be said at once that there is all the difference in the
world between the cults and the occult. The cults (which, as
distinct from new religions, are often called 'Christian devia-
tions') arise from a distortion or idiosyncratic interpretation
of Christianity. They express an aspiration for positive values
of various kinds, usually marked by excessive veneration of
an individual who is reckoned to be exceptionally gifted
spiritually. Usually devoted to a body of writings that are
placed on the same standing as the Bible, they are often
obsessed with an End-Times hope that envisages God very
soon taking direct rule over his creation. The values of the
cults are rival values to those of Christianity, often distortions
of it, but those who follow them do not, as a rule, do so

because they consider Christianity to be an empty joke, though they would certainly regard the established churches as failed enterprises and their own interpretation of Scripture the only valid one.

Very often, as Hoekema reminds us, those who are drawn into the cults are drawn in by good and positive aspects which the church ought to have been offering too, for they are part of the Christian gospel and the Christian world view. Thus, cult members and those who have left cults often testify to the warmth of the love they found expressed to them by other cult members; the strong feeling of community; the lack of materialism and desire to concentrate on spiritual matters; the outspoken condemnation by their leaders of many modern stupidities and heresies; the hunger for the Bible and other religious writings (admittedly, usually with a strong cult perspective); and often the integrity of the leadership. For every newspaper story of a Rev Moon living in luxury in America, there are a score of local cult leaders living in poverty and working strenuous long hours to bring their vision of a new world into being.

For a Christian, there is no true conversation possible between the beliefs of a cult and the biblical faith (though that is no reason to ostracise cult members socially or on a personal level). How can one reconcile a teaching that Jesus was not God, or that he left his task incomplete on the cross, or that salvation ultimately depends on your hard work for the gospel, with the clear teaching of the Bible? Personally I believe that side-by-side dialogue is always preferable to confrontational rhetoric, and I wish there were many more events such as the Unification-Evangelical Dialogues that have been held in the past. But such discussions have to be seen as debates between opposed, rival faith-commitments, not as policy meetings for fellow-believers.

It is sobering to remember what Irving Hexham and Myrtle Langley remind us of:

The vast majority of Moonies are intelligent, idealistic young people who have joined and remain in the movement by their own choice . . . not because they have been brainwashed but because they believe that the Unification Church holds the key to the salvation of the world.[2]

The testimony of many ex-cult members is that for them, the cult they joined seemed to offer spiritual nurture, truth and challenge that they had found lacking in the traditional churches which they had encountered. They did not want to be 'cult members' as such; they believed they had found the answer to all their questions, and therefore they followed the source of those answers. The case has rarely been put so poignantly as in a television drama many years ago which described a young woman, brainwashed into a cult by cult evangelists and brainwashed out of it by a professional 'de-programmer', who explained what the appeal had been of the charismatic visionary who had been the cult's leader: 'So he wasn't God after all,' she conceded. 'But tell me—who will save the world now?'

When we turn from the cults to the occult, we are looking at movements that by and large oppose, or discard, the church and operate by a different set of values. But as we have already seen, not every pagan member of occult religions by any means is worshipping the devil. Often their focus is on spiritual beings described as being, and serving, good; the concept of worshipping evil and totally inverting the Christian norms would be anathema to them. They would claim to be following a Way that predates Christianity and does not need the Christian revelation.

In the biblical view, there is no *absolute* difference between such beliefs and out-and-out satanism: 'He who is not with me is against me,' said Jesus, and the New Testament soberly points out many times that if you miss eternal salvation, the degree to which you missed it is not really much comfort to you. For the Christian the question must be, not 'What can the pagan revival offer me?' but 'What does the pagan revival teach me about what is lacking in my own Christian experience, which *ought* to be there if the Bible really is the authoritative guide to my faith and conduct?'

Let me suggest just three areas, out of many.

### The search for supernatural vitality

For many who become involved in today's pagan revival, the attraction is that they have found elements of religion that they have not found in their church, whether the fault be in the church or themselves. In an age when many churchmen publicly dispute central aspects of the Christian faith, when media scholarship tends frequently to disinter theories about Christian origins that are not new and have long ago been successfully challenged, but make excellent television, the pagan religions certainly offer one thing that has been sadly lacking in some churches: a conviction of the power and truth of the supernatural. A challenge that Francis Schaeffer and others have sometimes made to the Christian church goes like this: 'If the Holy Spirit were to disappear from the Christian gospel tomorrow—would it make any difference to your Christian experience?' A question (to quote the old Latin textbook) that sadly expects the answer 'No' . . .

In our materialistic age, dominated by the pursuit of things, there is a hunger for the supernatural which can only be met on a spiritual level, and some new pagan worshippers have said that for them that hunger is satisfied by their new-found religion in a way that no church which they knew could satisfy it. Such people certainly represent 'unpaid bills' of the church. In the Bible, Jesus pointed out that if you pray in faith, believing, then things actually happen (*cf.* Matt. 21:22). For some churches, and for some Christians, the verse might as well not be in the Bible at all. But there is not a coven in the land that does not believe implicitly in the *principle* underlying the verse, albeit in an altered or sometimes inverted context.

The pagan churches, right across the spectrum of paganism,

believe enthusiastically that religion means living in the supernatural dimension and expecting supernatural things to
happen. Sadly, many churches would be perplexed and somewhat inconvenienced if the supernatural intruded on their
customary ways of doing things.

## The Green imperative

Another area in which paganism is answering needs that
should have been addressed by churches but frequently have
not been, is the ecological debate that has been going on for
the past few years across the globe—the urge to save the
planet, to respect the environment, to hand on to the next
generation a world worth living in. In this respect movements
like the New Age movement and Christianity share some
major concerns:

> Although there are obviously some fundamental differences, there
> are also similarities in certain aspects of Christianity and New Age
> thought. Both reject the destructive, materialistic and utilitarian
> aspects of modern culture. Both believe in the need for radical
> transformation by individuals through a new world view. Many
> Christians agree with New Age followers that there is a need to
> think holistically rather than dualistically, to protect creation from
> exploitation, and to live in peaceful coexistence with others.[3]

The church, however, has had its share of ecologically
damaging projects, wasteful lifestyles, over-use of resources
and lack of concern for global issues (though there are some
voices, such as *Third Way* magazine and the Christian Impact
study centre in London, that have long argued for an informed
Christian platform on these issues). For some whose spiritual
interests include a major commitment to green issues, the
church's frequent failure to address such issues has made the
pagan movement an attractive option, especially that part of
it which is public and engaged in dialogue with the wider
community, for instance, the Druid organisations. A wiccan
priest expresses a sense of frustration and concern:

I think the time is coming now when we have to take the responsibility by the throat and actually get out there and say, 'There are answers here: I'm not prepared as a pagan, as a priest, and as a practising witch to sit back and see my planet, my mother, raped any longer.'[4]

## The search for spiritual roots

A third failure of which the established churches have sometimes been guilty is an inadequate sense of history. Often culturally hidebound, many churches are not only failing to relate to the present century, but are also failing to reflect any sense of historic Christendom, the church down the ages, the body of Christ that has existed on this earth since the days of his humanity and will go on existing until the earth and its heavens and all things are made new. Too often, church history is a record of disputes, and too many churches define themselves by a list of those from whom they differ.

Witchcraft, paganism and satanism certainly have their share of sectarianism and petty party squabbles (documented to some extent in John Parker's illuminating *At the Heart of Darkness*[5]), but the sense of antiquity implicit in most pagan movements is very strong: for example Druidism, with its doctrine of the sacred trust of the ancestral dead:

Druidry does not advocate spiritualism in the sense of communicating with the dead through trance-mediums, but it does teach us that we can look upon our ancestors, not as dead-and-gone, but as a rich resource that can provide us with a sense of connection to the world and to the life of humanity . . . When we know about our ancestors, when we sense them as living and as supporting us, then we feel connected to this genetic life-stream, and we draw strength and nourishment from this.[6]

There is much in the chapter by Philip Carr-Gomm from which this quotation is taken to give a biblical Christian cause for concern, but there is no doubt that many people today have a strong spiritual longing for a sense of contact with historic roots. It is a theme of many modern novels, for example Peter Ackroyd's *First Light* (1989), and the themes of heritage and chronicle are among the most pervasive in serious television.

The same fascination with origins has generated a massive publishing industry of which Erich von Däniken's *Chariots of the Gods?* (1969) was an early example: speculative, daring, often academically ludicrous, but offering breathtaking restructurings of how things came to be.

There exists, too, a modern tradition of occult rewritings of history in which the authors claimed to have understood the profound spiritual significance of previously unconsidered remnants of the past, this information having been given them by supernatural illumination. Authors writing in this way at various times include John Michell, T.C. Lethbridge and Alfred Watkins (most notably in his classic *The Old Straight Track*[7]). The Watkins tradition is developed (by Michell among others) in a number of ways: for example many who have written about Glastonbury Tor and other ancient sites have remarked on the supernatural vitality and interconnectedness of such places, and walking the ley-lines or ceremonially climbing the Tor both have religious significance for their followers. At this point, the reverence for the earth that many New Age thinkers demonstrate might be seen as a challenge—in several senses—to biblical Christianity's view of the created order.

Another example of the trend is the kind of historical writing exemplified by Immanuel Velikovsky, whose radical reinterpretations of antiquity, often involving a rewriting of cosmic as well as global history (eg *Worlds in Collision*, 1950) are to be found on the shelves of high street booksellers.

Yet another phenomenon is the extraordinary popularity of scientific and theoretical works that might seem to have a very limited market, but turn out to be best-sellers. This is partly because of the romantic appeal of pure theoretical thought in its own right (for example mathematics, music and propositional logic in Douglas Hofstadter[8]), or as the theme of a more traditional format (classical logic in Umberto Eco's mediaeval detective story[9]). But it is also because in the rarified discussion of post-Newtonian physics the same fascination with origins can be satisfied. This was demonstrated by the phenomenal success of Professor Stephen Hawking's *A Brief History of Time*[10]—whose author few academics (it is said) have the mental equipment to understand, and whose book is sometimes regarded as the least read bestseller of our age.

Mitchell, Lethbridge, Watkins and many more belong to a spirituality that finds in Hallowe'en, as in the whole seasonal cycle, a landmark and a point of spiritual energy. But the fascination with origins and the desire to draw spiritual strength and guidance from the past is not necessarily a bad thing. It is to be found in the Christian church, too. Such a fascination is found among groups such as the Evangelical Orthodox Church in America, one of whose leaders introduced an anthology of the ancient Church Fathers as follows:

> What Christian can help wondering what those people were like who received the gospel from the apostles? What must it have been like to live in those days of raw beginnings, struggle, and dire persecution? What sort of leaders did it take to bring the church through those early years when it was most tender and vulnerable? Wouldn't it be exciting to hear from those early leaders as they teach and interpret the Scriptures? . . . It is with a prayerful humility that these relics of our Fathers, who kept the faith and now cheer us on, are presented to you, the children.[11]

The words, while they have some similarity to those of Carr-Gomm quoted above, in fact encapsulate a fairly straightforward understanding of the Christian doctrine of the Communion of the Saints; and the last sentence in particular recalls the letter to the Hebrews, chapter 11 and 12:1.

At the present time there is a renewal of interest, among some protestants, in the Orthodox tradition and also in the old Celtic Church. A recently reprinted anthology of prayers in the Scottish celtic tradition was introduced with these words:

The reissue of this book witnesses to an encouraging growth of interest in Celtic spirituality. Our earliest Christian forefathers in Britain's 'Celtic crown' have so much to teach us; and a great deal of our contemporary malaise stems from a neglect of their balanced grasp of the gospel message.[12]

The theme is the same; that in the past lies a rich treasury of spiritual wisdom and understanding, and, if we would only tap it, it has the power to bring clarity and wisdom into our modern confused and sometimes directionless life. In 1992, finding myself at a conference in which there was much use of Celtic spirituality and worship patterns—and considerable use of Celtic approaches to apologetics in a number of the seminars—I asked some of the participants what the attraction of the old Celtic church was for them. 'It is a tradition that stands outside both Protestant and Catholic, Eastern and Western,' they said. 'It's a way of reaching back to the beginning, of finding another Christian way.'

## Hallowe'en: the alternative celebration?

For a Christian believer, there is nothing in paganism that offers an acceptable alternative to Christianity. The reason does not lie in paganism but in Christianity. There can be no co-existence between Christ and other deities, be they tree-spirits, the wise Old Ones, demons or even Satan himself.

Jesus answered, 'I am the way and the truth and the life. No one comes to the Father except through me.' (John 14:6)

There can be no other king. Yet whatever else the rise of paganism and the spread of occult interest and practitioners indicates, it points in some cases at least to shortcomings in the church's preaching and living.

Every year, the celebration of Hallowe'en involves a good deal of expensive trivia and a mountain of media exploitation, but at the heart are a small core of people who celebrate Hallowe'en with the same reverence that Christians celebrate Easter. It is a depressing commentary on the state of much of

the Western Christian church that many of them do so
because they have found in paganism a spiritual quality
lacking in the churches.

Yet I would like to appeal to those who may be members
of that minority, who have rejected biblical Christianity in the
past for reasons such as those mentioned above. You may
have tried very hard to fit in to a local church that did not
seem much interested in you and whose teaching was dry and
powerless. It may well be that in paganism or some other
religious belief you have found the spiritual energy, power
and conviction, the lack of which was the very thing that drove
you away from the churches. Perhaps you were alienated by
the other-worldliness, the pseudo-spirituality—sometimes the
ugliness—in which worship was conducted, and the absence
of any sense that behind all the ritual and complication was a
truth and a living God who might conceivably be interested
in you and want to cherish you and love you. And some of
what you failed to find in church you have found elsewhere.

But I would ask you to bear in mind your experiences in
paganism, too. If you are a member of a pagan community or
church then you are used to public ridicule, to assumptions
that all who claim the title 'witch' are evil-doers, bizarre
freaks, warped minds, perhaps even child molesters. You will
surely have encountered much that is counterfeit and much
that is glamourised. If you have found any good thing at all
in paganism, you had to sift through a great deal of media
misrepresentation, lies and misunderstanding to find it. In the
occult and arcane world there are many individuals who are
no credit to your movement, and some who revolt good
people of any persuasion. You refused to accept them as
typical.

I would simply ask you to look at Christianity with the same
persistence. The Christian churches too have their bizarre
publicists, their moribund congregations, their materialists
and their snobs. The pagan world has no monopoly on misuse
of spiritual gifts. There are thousands of living, growing,
spiritually healthy Christian churches, but it is not difficult

to find also cold churches, dead churches, environmentally disastrous churches and churches that adulterate the Christian gospel with rubbish that does not belong to it. In this, too, it is necessary to sift and test.

For what lies at the heart of Christianity is not a spiritual code but a spiritual Being: the infinite, personal God, revealed in the person of Jesus Christ and active in this world in the work of the Holy Spirit. All else (as Queen Elizabeth the First once remarked) is a dispute about trifles. A person's relationship to the Creator God through his Son Jesus Christ the Redeemer is the most important single issue in the universe. Even if you have been distracted by the failings of a fallible church and its fallible members, that issue is much too important to be left unresolved.

CHAPTER TEN

# ALTERNATIVE CELEBRATIONS

Suppose that after carefully considering the history and implications of Hallowe'en we decide that it is a festival we no longer wish to observe. This may be an individual decision; it may be a family decision; it may also be a decision made by a school.

It will not be easy, for Hallowe'en has, in a relatively short time, established itself in Western society, and if you opt out there may be protests, especially if, as some have, you make it a local campaign. Business interests will not be pleased; local shops benefit from Hallowe'en trade, the media revel in it, and there is considerable money invested at every level. Your neighbours may not be too pleased either, if you decline to be involved in trick'n'treating. In your own family, your children will be subject to peer pressure from their friends who will want them to join in the Hallowe'en fun, and in school you may have to decide what to do if your child's class is required to get involved in a Hallowe'en exercise.

Such a decision is, in a real sense, a battle. It may be an open battle; one Christian shopkeeper in a North of England town who wrote a piece in his local newspaper, criticising Hallowe'en and suggesting that it be abandoned, received threatening telephone calls from people claiming to be witches and found his shop front daubed with occult slogans.

It will certainly be a hidden battle, for the battle that the Bible describes as being waged perpetually between good and evil is fought over this ground too. A Christian cannot see Hallowe'en as other than a night in which the devil is given free reign, whether his symbols are treated as harmless fun or whether he is actively worshipped.

His victories are not only those represented by the Church of Satan and similar organisations. A Christian studying the writings and rituals of many 'white' witches and pagans will often find much that is beautiful and moving, much that has a note of reverence for the earth and a longing for spiritual reality that will find an echo in his or her own heart. But the tragedy for a Christian is that so many have gone only part of the way towards truth.

It was the great chess player Emanuel Lasker who, in the context of discussing the best move in a chess game, observed that the enemy of the good was not the bad but the almost-good. In researching this book and handling some of the material for several years, my own greatest sadness as a Christian has not been the filthy blasphemies of the World-wide Church of Satan, but the many thoughtful, gentle people who have rejected the gospel of Jesus Christ in favour of the gospel of paganism. In biblical terms, that is no gospel at all; and in the spiritual battle, those who have been blinded are as much casualties as those who deliberately refused to look at the truth.

But let us suppose that you decide to go ahead and remove the festival of Hallowe'en from your lives. It's a decision that I and my family have made, as have many others. For example, Rev. Richard Thomas, Communications Officer for the Diocese of Oxford:

> We as a family have taken a decision that we won't celebrate Hallowe'en and that our children won't take part in Hallowe'en celebrations. Not particularly because the festival itself is some-thing to be avoided but because of the associations that have become attached to it which I think are unhealthy for all sorts of reasons.
>
> I think there is sometimes, though not always, an association with the occult. Being a witch is something we are told quite

specifically in the Bible to avoid. Also, I think that to collude with that kind of festival is to give the impression 'Well, you know—it's only a bit of fun'; but it can sometimes go beyond that. Some of the Hallowe'en masks are pretty horrific. It's the other side of what the Bible calls 'all things good, true, honourable, healthy, holy' . . . and I don't really want my children associating with that. Then the aspect of trick and treat concerns me. It can be like obtaining goods by menaces—'Unless you give me something I'm going to do harm to your house or something.' It may be just a chalk sign on the wall, but we've had things done which have been difficult to clean off, because we were not home on All Hallows Eve. What does that do to the child? Does it teach that it's all right to obtain things by threat? I don't find that aspect healthy.[1]

On the other hand, Hallowe'en is a dominating theme of our society, one of the media, commercial and social highlights of Autumn. It is impossible to leave the house from early October onwards without being aware of the fact that Hallowe'en is almost upon us. Children especially, in their comics, magazines and TV programmes are encouraged to look forward to it, and schools often incorporate Hallowe'en themes in activities, class projects and occasionally formal work projects.

How, then, can an alternative be put forward—one that will celebrate the good themes (such as the seasonal cycles and the theme of death and rebirth that focuses on the harvest/autumn element in the traditional druidical Hallowe'en celebration) that are present in the traditional festival, but will avoid at the same time celebrating the destructive and unhelpful elements?

The Association of Christian Teachers has put forward constructive, creative suggestions for alternative celebrations. Advising parents wishing to object to Hallowe'en in schools, they suggest (1) that the arguments against Hallowe'en be presented 'with as much clarity and courtesy as possible, bearing in mind that Hallowe'en is usually introduced without much reflection on what it means'; (2) that parents should be prepared to put the case against Hallowe'en to the press, 'at least to encourage some thought before it is celebrated as a mindless custom'; and (3) that, if it is not possible to stop Hallowe'en being observed in the school, 'it is possible to make the best of it by portraying the destruction of evil and the triumph of good. This is what the Christian festival of All Hallows did at its best.'[2]

In the ACT leaflet *'Allo 'Allo, it's HALLOWE'EN again!*, Margaret Cooling makes the further point that there are educational grounds for not celebrating Hallowe'en:

> It is not part of any mainstream faith: it is rather a relic of our pagan past. The curriculum is very full and a subject such as Hallowe'en takes up valuable curriculum time that could be devoted to topics which are educationally more worthwhile. One of the main reasons for using Hallowe'en in schools is the creative stimulus it gives. Hallowe'en is a very good context for creative writing, poetry and art. There are other, better, creative stimuli.[3]

## Alternative school activities

Some of these stimuli are described in the short inexpensive booklet written by Margaret Cooling, *Hallowe'en in the Classroom?*, which I strongly recommend to parents, teachers and school governors as a professional teacher's contribution to devising alternative celebrations (see p. 142). She suggests five topics, and gives useful advice on implementing them in a classroom situation.

The first makes use of the fact that the last week in October has been designated as *One World Week*. The project 'aims to introduce children to the concepts of diversity, unity and dependence', and the booklet shows how the theme can be explored in interesting and creative ways in such disciplines as music, art, creative writing, religious education, drama and geography. Schools exploring this project will be transformed into a colourful bazaar of different nations, and the underlying issues of human interdependence and global brotherhood/sisterhood are well set out in the teaching suggestions.

The second topic is on the theme of *'opposites'*, taking up the theme of good and evil as polarised, and uses it as a starting point for looking at the Christian festival of All Hallows. Again, teachers' notes are provided indicating how the theme of opposites can be explored through art, movement, PSE and other school subjects. The theme of All Hallows is developed by suggestions that Christian saints or other famous Christians be studied, and the evils against which they fought: thus Mother Teresa might be taken as a special topic for study and project work.

The third project takes up another All Hallows theme, that of *remembrance*: 'All Hallows is a time when the good are remembered, and when right prevails, when heroes and heroines are honoured.' There are useful suggestions for class activities in general project work, such as an investigation of the various ways in which people remember and the way we use memorials and anniversaries. In religious education, the theme is applied to Passover and Easter in interesting and stimulating ways, and there are some suggestions for further reading.

The fourth project specifically considers the Christian festivals of *All Saints and All Hallows*. This involves investigating local saints, exploring place names, looking at symbols used in religious art and, in music, looking at hymns and songs about saints. Mediaeval saints' lives are used as the starting point for an exploration of calligraphy, and instructions are given for making simple banners. This project emphasises class participation, especially in musical activities.

The last project is on *The Middle Ages*, and has the potential to involve work in a wide variety of subjects, on such topics as clothes, food, work, daily life, education, farming, castles and the Black Death. The seasonal emphasis of Hallowe'en is reflected in the suggestion that Michaelmas be celebrated (late) at the end of October in its place. Falling on 29 September, it shares Hallowe'en's sense of the year dying and being reborn. It was the time when, for example, labourers' contracts expired, and people stood in the market place wearing symbols of their job hoping to find employment for the next year. This is a fruitful source of ideas for projects: Margaret Cooling suggests that children might try staging their own fair, devising their own costumes and job symbols including some to represent twentieth-century occupations. The traditional view of St Michael as the champion of good over evil is used in the project as the basis for a positive underlying ethos of the power of good and the praiseworthiness of love.

Any of these ideas could be used to devise class projects, small or large, that would provide at least as strong creative and educational stimulus as Hallowe'en projects. Although guidance is provided for applying the themes to religious education, they could be used successfully by teachers of other subjects, and could readily be adapted for use in schools that, while disliking the Hallowe'en festival, did not wish to promote Christianity.

## Church alternatives

I write as a Christian and a member of a Christian church. However, I am very aware that Hallowe'en is sometimes a problem for members of other faiths, and I hope that these comments which are addressed to Christians will be of help in other contexts.

In churches, there is often a range of opinion about Hallowe'en, especially where the congregation includes Americans. The custom of trick'n'treat, for example, is extremely popular in America and is often regarded as a harmless activity that has nothing to do with any larger issues. In a sense this is quite right; we would be a much poorer world if every folk tradition that had no useful or moral purpose were to be eradicated, and there is an element of fun in Hallowe'en which we need to recognise. Christianity is not a faith that is opposed to fun *per se*. However, it is often true that Christians have not thought very much about the overall implications of Hallowe'en, and it is very difficult indeed to separate the fun aspect from the larger issues we have been discussing.

A useful exercise to begin with in churches, therefore, is to organise a discussion around the subject perhaps with the aim of preparing a common approach to local schools, shops and other agencies promoting Hallowe'en. Participants in the discussion should be given some preliminary material such as a list of Bible passages and perhaps some of the information presented in this book and in others.

It is a very good idea to organise a church service or other activity on the night of Hallowe'en itself: apart from any other consideration, if we believe that Hallowe'en is a night when evil is abroad and is actively courted (knowingly or unknowingly), then the need to pray and think together as a church about the situation is paramount. But it is quite possible to organise an event which is a celebration and which will be so attractive that it will dissuade some from attending the Hallowe'en events going on at the same time. It should be a family event, and it might well be a time of building up the church family in good and positive ways. The church might join together to produce a dramatic presentation such as *Mr Goodlight*, described below; this could bring together several generations of the church and use a variety of skills.

There are other activities that can be explored, all of which shift the emphasis away from the Hallowe'en theme. One local fellowship group of a church I know, whose members were concerned at the high profile of Hallowe'en in the local schools and in the media, decided to hold a simple communion service on that night. And Margaret Cooling's point that sometimes it is possible to make the best of it even when Hallowe'en events go ahead is a good one. One parent, faced with an invitation for their child to attend a Hallowe'en party, was concerned at the imagery and theme of the party— children were asked to come dressed as witches—but felt it would be wrong to forbid her child to go. After considerable thought and prayer she sent her daughter dressed as a good fairy. This preserved the relationship with the birthday child's family, diluted the overall theme of the party, and opened up a discussion in an amicable way.

For Hallowe'en 1992, several neighbouring churches in Abingdon joined together in an evening of activities called 'Five to Midnight', which involved the young people and focused on positive themes. It was organised by David Bryan, Curate of Christ Church Abingdon:

> For me the great problem is that Hallowe'en celebrates things that are not good and focuses on aspects of humanity that are not good. It appeals to the cruel streak in us. Hallowe'en humour, for example, is often cruel. It's another side of the darkness; not so much to do with having fun, but appealing to what is best not encouraged. And there's a possibility, too, of getting involved in the occult; not all do get involved, of course, but for some it goes far beyond mischief-making. So we wanted to turn the emphasis in another direction, to focus on what is good and to look for ways in which God can help us to live better lives and make a better contribution to the lives of those around us.[4]

## The Mr Goodlight Show

The following account of a presentation produced by the CROPS Trust (Christian Options in Peterborough Schools) is included here by permission. While it does not claim to be a professional production, it is packed with ideas for others to copy.

This 'low-key evangelistic event' is a 'musical/games evening/activity' that grew out of a series of alternative Hallowe'en events for Christian youngsters organised by the Peterborough Youth for Christ movement during the late 1980s and early 1990s. In 1991 it was decided that the young people should be more outward-looking, and as a result Richard Morrison wrote *Mr Goodlight and his Rainbow Mirrors*, which was performed in eight locations to about 1,000 children at Hallowe'en 1991 under the slogan 'Your brightest Hallowe'en ever!'.

The production (which is intended for Junior Schools) uses young actors, musicians, singers and one person who operates a spotlight. Other members of the team are dispersed around the hall, acting as helpers to the audience who are divided up into small groups. The storyline tells how fear of the dark can be overcome if one has a friend. The concept of friendship is explored in group exercises and songs, and the central character is introduced: Mr Goodlight, who is a simple parable of Jesus Christ. He talks about the life and work of Jesus in terms of light conquering darkness, and invites the children to learn more about him and follow him.

The evangelism is explicit (the children are offered evangelistic leaflets as they go home), but acceptable in the context of school assemblies and religious education.

The activities are interesting and contribute to the theme: for example, blindfolds are used in the 'Recognising people' and 'Doing it in the dark competition' activities. In the former, the purpose is to demonstrate to the children how much easier it is to recognise people from touching them, talking to them and finally seeing them for who they really are; in the second, blindfolded pairs of contestants have to attach clothespegs to each other and remove them. In both, the point is gently underlined by the leader to make sure that everybody understands.

The songs are bright and catchy, and have a strong singalong flavour.

*Mr Goodlight* is an excellent example of how amateurs can produce an entertaining and meaningful alternative to Hallowe'en without spending a great deal of money and without involving a large number of people in lengthy preparations (in the performances so far the parts have been read from scripts rather than memorised, and scenery is extremely simple). The author, Richard Morison, is willing to make copies of the script and associated material available to anybody interested.[5] Hopefully it will be an incentive for others to produce similar products.

### Going public: writing to the newspapers

One option available to anybody who wants to make a public issue of a problem is to write to the press. The letter pages of most local newspapers are a recognised forum for all sorts of discussions, and editors are usually open to receiving letters on any conceivable topic. Hallowe'en is often the subject for vigorous debate in local and national newspapers. Some guidelines for successful letter writing on this, as on other subjects, are:

*Keep your letter brief and light.* The kind of letter that goes on for several columns is boring to read and is less likely to be accepted. Often such letters appear in print having been substantially edited, and the writer has no control over what is left out. If you really want to write at length, it may be worth asking the editor if he or she would be prepared to publish an item in the main pages, perhaps under the 'Christian comment' or similar column.

*Organise your thoughts.* Make one point in each paragraph and order your paragraphs so that the points they make are cumulative. Don't be sidetracked, don't be tempted to make throw-away comments or gratuitous insults to people with whom you disagree, and do concentrate on your main argument.

*Woo your readers.* Most of the readers will be uninterested in your opposition to Hallowe'en; it is not a subject that is widely discussed, despite the rise of interest in the festival and the corresponding rise of disquiet. Try to choose aspects of the problem that will arouse the interest of general readers: the commercial exploitation, the potential for emotional stress to children, etc.

*Don't speak as of right.* The newspaper is a forum, not a pulpit. You are standing on a soapbox in a market place of ideas; you will have to earn the right to have your views respected. Do not harangue your readers for not sharing your faith, and especially do not assume that because somebody sees no harm in introducing children to Hallowe'en entertainments, they are therefore intent on corrupting children.

## Other Platforms

One of the false assumptions often made about modern media is that they are one-way, and that we are all doomed to be non-participating consumers. In fact there are a number of ways one can join in media debates apart from the obvious one of competing for the editor's attention on the newspaper letters page.

*Television audience debates* such as *Kilroy* and *The Time, the Place* . . . usually announce the subjects of forthcoming programmes in advance and invite members of the public to attend, asking people with a particular interest in the subject to write in for tickets. Once in the studio, you will find that a seat in the audience does not guarantee an opportunity to speak, but careful viewing of several programmes beforehand will give you a feel for the most effective way to present your argument.

*Television producers* and other people responsible for programmes are well known to pay considerable attention to letters from the public. A telephone call to the Duty Officer, too, will always be noted and passed on to the people concerned. It is as important to commend what is good as to criticise what is bad; sadly most people who are active letter-writers to television devote themselves entirely to criticism. A good example of how to argue with television is provided by the various programmes presented by James Whale for ITV.

Sometimes called the rudest man on television (in the sense of bad manners!), Whale is actually willing to allow almost anybody to set out their stall in his marketplace of ideas and argue their case. What he will not tolerate is pomposity, bad argument, name-calling and stupidity: quite a few spokes-persons for Christian causes, currently licking their wounds after an encounter with him, probably regard James Whale as virulently anti-Christian. However, a number of articulate, forthright and courteous Christians have been allowed to dominate several of his programmes because they presented their case effectively. He does not always get it right (a recent debate on abortion was a shambles) but generally speaking his programmes are very worthwhile.

*Radio programmes* are another way in which one's voice can be heard; phone-ins on national and local radio are open to everybody, though the more popular subjects may mean that the phone lines are jammed for most of the programme. Radio, and television too, offers the opportunity for the public to make their own programmes: television's community film units and radio's talks and features departments can provide information; details can be obtained from *Radio Times* and other programme listings. Another feature both radio and television offer is audience feedback programmes; Channel 4's *Right to Reply* is particularly effective and is open to any viewer; details of how to make your voice heard on this and other similar radio and television programmes can be found either in *Radio Times* or from the programmes themselves.

*   *   *

If you believe that the time has come to abandon Hallowe'en as a public festival, these are resources which should be used to help to generate public debate on the matter and challenge those who argue that Hallowe'en is just trivial, meaningless fun.

To campaign for the abolition of Hallowe'en *entirely* is not the same thing, and the case for doing so is a very unclear one. In a pluralist society, we should be very cautious before prohibiting anybody the right to exercise their religious convictions; to prevent witches from holding Hallowe'en as a religious festival would not only be tantamount to restoring the old witchcraft laws but would also be highly inconsistent. Paganism is incontrovertibly a religion. It is not a religion with which I agree; as a Christian, I would like more than anything to see paganism eradicated, because it preaches a gospel which I believe to be eclipsed and repudiated by the biblical gospel of Jesus Christ. But the same is true of the Muslim faith, of the Jewish faith and of the Jehovah's Witness faith, to name only three religious movements that would challenge Christianity's central creed that Jesus is the risen Lord and Saviour of the world, and that beside him there is no other. If paganism is to be outlawed, how can one with consistency and integrity allow *any* non-Christian faith to operate?

The legal right of Druids to worship at Stonehenge, of witches to celebrate on sabbats, and similar religious freedoms is unanswerable. So long as such groups in their turn observe the law (and I would think that photographs issued by the Church of Satan would in Britain at least provide grounds for a police investigation under the legislation that is designed to protect minors) they are legally entitled to practise their religion undisturbed. This principle must not be obscured by the fact that, as is apparent from the sources quoted in this book, some pagan movements would seem to have broken the law in a number of ways.

But acceptance (even defence, where necessary) of the civil and legal rights of others is quite a different matter to the celebration of Hallowe'en throughout the Western world as a public festival.

Those for whom Hallowe'en has a spiritual significance are a small minority in our society. They are entitled to practise their beliefs peaceably, but it is quite wrong to impose those beliefs on the rest of society. To be fair, few of them, in this case, do. The overwhelming weight of Hallowe'en promotion in the West comes from people who place no spiritual value on the festival at all, but are using it as an occasion for fun or profiting financially from its exploitation.

In that context the historic legacy of Hallowe'en deserves to be scrutinised. How much do we wish to make a national festival of what historically has so often been associated with the darker side of human nature, with violence and cruelty, and with the satanic calendar? Such associations of the festival, and the wider considerations we have outlined in this book, have led many Christians to see the Hallowe'en issue as a matter for spiritual warfare. I would agree with them. To the various resources suggested above should be added the spiritual resources given us to equip us for that warfare.

A church or other group of believers seeing a rise in occult activity on the neighbourhood should commit itself to urgent, hard-working, believing prayer. Individuals should make it their business to find out what is being taught and practised, and to make contact and talk with individuals involved. A popular exercise, and one with great value, is 'prayer-walking', in which a group of Christians walk through an area claiming it for Christ and praying for the district as they walk. It may seem bizarre to some Christians, but may well seem more sensible when one realises how many pagan and occult movements do exactly the same thing in an attempt to win their area to their beliefs. Where there is satanic and other occult activity, especially in schools, it may be necessary to call in the help of Christians with a particular ministry of deliverance; if such problems are happening in your area, the two videos mentioned in the reading list at the end of this book will be helpful.

As a positive response, the alternatives we have looked at in this chapter—and many more like them that can easily be devised—are well worth considering. The theme of death and rebirth, for example, is central to many faiths beside Christianity, and could be an acceptable basis for an autumn festival in schools and other institutions that would be immensely enjoyable for both children and adults. For the Christian, what better time to celebrate the Creator God and the Lord Jesus Christ through whom 'everything that was made, has been made', than the turning of the year as it swings from fruitfulness into its long sleep, with the prospect of bursting into life again in the Spring's new birth? It is a traditional Hallowe'en theme, and also one celebrated by many Christian writers: here is Episcopalian minister and exuberant chef Robert Farrar Capon, meditating on the vineyard harvest:

How much better a world it becomes when you see Him creating at all times and at every time; when you see that the preserving of the old in being is just as much creation as the bringing of the new out of nothing. Each thing, at every moment, becomes the

delight of His hand, the apple of His eye. The bloom of yeast
lies upon the grapeskins year after year because He likes it;
$C_6H_{12}O_6=2C_2H_5OH+2CO_2$ is a dependable process because,
every September, He says, That was nice; do it again.[6]

It is only in very recent times that Hallowe'en has been a
widely celebrated festival. The time may well have come to
allow it to disappear back into the history books, in much the
same way that Guy Fawkes' night is changing as the rising
costs and safety concerns are turning it from a family to a
community occasion, with the historical association much
diminished.

As with Guy Fawkes night, one can expect business interests
to view the prospect with dismay and opposition. In the
American video *Halloween: Trick or Treat*, presenter Chuck
Smith offers a few statistics from the USA: a department store
chain selling half a billion dollars' worth of Hallowe'en
merchandise in the five weeks leading up to the festival;
theatrical costume shops that only break even because of the
Hallowe'en trade; a farmer planting a 164-acre field with
pumpkins for an anticipated $200,000 profit. There are also
secondary markets such as candy for trick'n'treat, and of
course the huge Hollywood Hallowe'en industry. But why
should an unhealthy festival be kept simply to satisfy business
interests?

There is nothing so precious about Hallowe'en that it must
be preserved at all costs; and what is worth celebrating would
certainly survive the disappearance of the festival.

# THE ILEA INSPECTORATE REPORT

*ILEA Inspectors' Warning on Occultism in Schools*
To: Head Teachers in all Schools
March 1986

Dear Colleague,
The Education Officer receives a small but continuous stream of letters from parents who are concerned that their children's interest in the occult is being stimulated by aspects of their education. This may involve reading schemes which involve ghosts, teaching about witches, computer games with a strong 'fear' element, celebration of Hallowe'en and direct teaching about the occult. Something of the anxiety of parents may be gauged by the fact that a Christian organisation has just published and completely sold 50,000 copies of a pamphlet called *Danger Children at Play* within four weeks.

We have therefore met as an Inspectorate Committee to consider the matter and believe it would be helpful if we registered our concerns so that you may bear them in mind when deciding on your own policies.

1. We are concerned about INACCURACY. Many stories of witches, for example, fail to inform children that the term was often applied to women who lived alone and who were victims of superstition and cruelty.
2. We are concerned about the heightening of CHILDREN'S FEARS. Although there is a view that when children's fears

are stimulated by frightening stories in a controlled setting, it enables them to learn to face fears outside of such support, we are aware of children who have been badly frightened by stories and other activities, even to the point when it has caused severely disturbed behaviour.

3. We are concerned about INSENSITIVITY. Many religious believers (Christians, Jews and Muslims for example) believe that there is a spiritual reality which lies behind this world and that there are forces of evil as well as good. They believe that it is possible for children's interest in the occult to be stimulated by games, festivities and stories which involve some kind of emotional reaction to the occult and that it is harmful to their children. They are not generally opposed to objective teaching about such elements—indeed this might be an important element in education—but they are concerned at what they feel to be encouragement or endorsing of occult practices.

We hope these points will help you in what appears to be a growing area of concern.

Yours sincerely . . .

Note—the above is a document prepared by the *Inspectorate*, not the Education Authority itself.

# FOR FURTHER READING

The following publications have been of particular help in writing this book, though a large number of others have also been consulted, some of which appear in the notes. Not all the titles listed can be recommended to all readers without reservation; some are included as resources for those with a particular concern for the subject.

## Paganism and the occult

As explained earlier, the present book is not a detailed study of either subject. I have found two books particularly useful as reference sources:

David Burnett, *Dawning of the Pagan Moon* (MARC Monarch, 1991). This is a substantial investigation into various facets of the renaissance of pagan belief in recent years. Scrupulously fair, thoroughly researched and making use of extensive interviews with representatives of various groups, the author gives a straightforward description of pagan beliefs and presents his own commitment to Christianity as a convincing and powerful rejection of the pagan gospel.

John Parker, *At the Heart of Darkness: Witchcraft, Black Magic and Satanism Today* (Sidgwick & Jackson, 1993). John Parker is an experienced journalist who has personally attended rituals described in the book and has interviewed key figures. Though sceptical about many of the claims of some Christian lobbies, he argues that there is a growing and disturbing network of occult practitioners and worshippers active today. Some readers may find the information and illustrations distressing.

## Hallowe'en, the festival

Margaret Cooling, *'Allo 'Allo, it's HALLOWE'EN again!* (Association of Christian Teachers, 1988). A 4-page leaflet intended for use in house groups and church study groups, though it could be used for individual study. The title, referring to the popular television comedy, alludes to the central argument of the leaflet.

Margaret Cooling, *Hallowe'en* (Association of Christian Teachers, [1982]). This 4-page leaflet briefly sets out a balanced case against Hallowe'en and gives some biblical guidance on the subject, together with suggestions for discussing the matter with schools.

Margaret Cooling, *Hallowe'en in the Classroom?* (Association of Christian Teachers, 1988). Now out of print, see below.

Richard Wilkins, *Hallowe'en in Schools* (Association of Christian Teachers, 1993). This is a revision and expansion of Margaret Cooling's *Hallowe'en in the Classroom?*, including the class project ideas that are described in Chapter 10. It incorporates additional material on alternative festivals and other topics. Highly recommended.

(ACT publications are obtainable from: Association of Christian Teachers, 2 Romeland Hill, St Albans, Herts AL3 4ET.)

Antony Ewens, *Hallowe'en, All Souls' and All Saints'* (Religious and Moral Education Press: Living Festivals series, 1983). This is an attractively-produced 32-page booklet that summarises the history of the three festivals and describes some of their features and traditions. It is usefully illustrated and simply written, and would make a useful teaching aid.

Ewens takes a fairly liberal view of Hallowe'en; he describes the pagan origins but points out that Christians reject many of the implications of the Hallowe'en traditions. He provides suggestions for scary activities and frightening masks, all of a traditional nature.

## Other resources

Philip Carr-Gomm, *The Elements of the Druid Tradition* (Element Books, 1991). Mr Carr-Gomm is Chief of the Order of Bards, Ovates and Druids. His book is easily available, well written and covers a wide range of druidic history and teaching.

James G. Frazer, *The Golden Bough: a Study in Magic and Religion* (Abridged version 1922: I have used the St Martin's Library edition). Frazer abridged his own massive work and thus achieved a wide readership—helped by the poet T.S. Eliot's publicising of the book in the notes to *The Waste Land*. Frazer's work needs to be handled with care, and he tends to document his references poorly.

T.D. Kendrick, *The Druids: a Study in Keltic Prehistory* (Methuen, 2nd edn 1928). Kendrick is well spoken of by Carr-Gomm and his book is a classic study of the subject. However, his discussion of Hallowe'en is taken very substantially from J.G. Frazer's *The Golden Bough*, see above.

Lewis Spence, *The Magic Arts in Celtic Britain* (Dorset Press, 1992). The author, a member of the Royal Anthropological Institute and an expert on Celtic culture, provides a comprehensive survey. Spence's work is quoted by John Parker (above) as being objective and critical, though he is firmly committed to the Celtic vision of life.

## Videos

*Halloween: Trick or Treat*: 56 minutes (The Pagan Invasion, Vol.1: Cutting Edge/Jeremiah Films, 1990). Jeremiah Films UK, PO Box 26, Bicester, Oxfordshire. This American

Christian video (obviously intended for showing on American TV stations, as it has irritating breaks to allow commercials to be inserted) includes contributions from witches and satanists and shows actual occult rituals, judiciously edited for nudity etc. A glossy hi-tech production, it features well-known Christian teacher Chuck Smith and others. It uses the non-Christian contributions quite responsibly, and goes into its various topics in some depth. It is really more of a discussion of the pagan/occult revival than a video specifically about Hallowe'en, though Hallowe'en is given special emphasis.

*Doorways to Danger*: 25 minutes (Sunrise Video, n.d., 1990?) Doorways to Danger, PO Box 437, Worthing, West Sussex BN14 8AL. 'This video explains why it is dangerous to get involved with spiritism, fortune telling, witchcraft/magic and satanism.' The significance of Hallowe'en for satanists is spelt out in the course of a low-key, informal presentation of the Christian view of the occult. Topics are dealt with briefly, sometimes too sketchily—the material on fantasy is especially weak. But it's a good discussion starter for schools and groups, especially as the title reflects an emphasis on the dangers of playing with ouija boards and other occult paraphernalia. A study guide is included.

# NOTES

## Chapter 1

1 E. Cobhan Brewer, *The Dictionary of Phrase and Fable* (1870: Avenel Books edn, 1978), p. 573.

2 Joyce M. Hawkins (comp.) *Oxford Current English Dictionary* (OUP, 1990).

3 Joseph Strutt, *The Sports and Pastimes of the People of England* (1801: ed. William Hone, 1849), p. 391.

4 Iona and Peter Opie, *The Lore and Language of Schoolchildren* (Oxford University Press, 1959), p. 274.

5 It's worth establishing at the outset that the word 'pagan' will not be used in this book in a colloquial or pejorative way, but as a precise term of comparative religion, taking seriously the rise of an articulate, committed and often proselytising body of pagan worshippers in Britain and the post-Christian West in general. This renaissance of paganism is very well analysed in David Burnett, *Dawning of the Pagan Moon: an Investigation into the Rise of Western Paganism* (MARC/Monarch, 1991).

6 Cf. Nigel Pennick, *Practical Magic of the Northern Tradition* (1989), quoted in David Burnett, *op. cit.* p. 156.

7 Bruno Bettelheim, *A Good Enough Parent: the Guide to Bringing up your Child* (Thames and Hudson, 1987: Pan edn 1988), p. 374f.

8 William Schnoebelen, *Wicca: Satan's Little White Lie* (Chick Publications, 1990) Schnoebelen's credentials as an ex-wiccan high priest command respect, and he is writing in the American context; but in the British context too much research has been published to deny that there is a substantial body of pagan and

occult belief that is not satanist and does not seek to invert Christianity even though it opposes it (Schnoebelen extends, not very helpfully, Jesus' statement 'He that is not for me is against me' to mean that all non-Christians are thereby satanists, p. 206).

## Chapter 2

1 James G. Frazer, *The Golden Bough: a Study in Magic and Religion* (abr. edn, 1922). Sir James Frazer (1854–1941) was a classical scholar whose major work was in this area. His basic premise—that communities pass from magic to religion and thence to science—has little credibility today, but the importance of his work as a gatherer of information is acknowledged.
2 Frazer (p. 829) suggests that the Celtic festivals do however reflect the farming year.
3 Charles Kightly, *The Customs and Ceremonies of Britain* (1986), p. 132.
4 Frazer, *op. cit.* p. 830.
5 Philip Carr-Gomm, *The Elements of the Druid Tradition* (Element Books, 1991), p. 70.
6 T.D. Kendrick, *The Druids: a Study in Keltic Prehistory* (2nd edn, 1928), p. 130. See original texts for Kendrick's documentation of his sources. Kendrick acknowledges—and borrows heavily from—J.G. Frazer's work on Hallowe'en.
7 Both are recorded contributions to the video *Hallowe'en: Trick or Treat* (Jeremiah U.K.)
8 Henry Chadwick, 'The Spread and Structure of the Early Church', in: Henry Chadwick and G.R. Evans, *Atlas of the Christian Church* (Macmillan, 1987), p. 30.
9 Antony Ewens, *Hallowe'en, All Souls' and All Saints'* (Religious and Moral Education Press, 1983), p. 18.
10 Charles Neil and J.M. Willoughby (eds), *The Tutorial Prayer Book* (Church Book Room Press, 1963), p. 208.
11 Antony Ewens, *op. cit.*, p. 22.
12 Iona and Peter Opie, *The Lore and Language of Schoolchildren* (Oxford University Press, 1959), p. 275.

## Chapter 3

1 Heather Sharpe, 'Pear Tree of Knowledge', *Times Educational Supplement* (23 October 1992), p. 12. It should be noted that

the article goes on to give a more positive view of Hallowe'en fantasy and the passage quoted does not reflect the thrust of the article.

2 Issued by the ILEA Inspectorate, March 1986: included in Margaret Cooling, *'Allo 'Allo, it's HALLOWE'EN again* (Association of Christian Teachers, 1988), p. 3. The Inspectorate's document is reproduced in full as Appendix 1 of the present book.

3 John Gilbert, 'Dark Playground', in *Fear* No. 4 (Jan–Feb 1989), p. 5.

4 A year or so ago I was in correspondence with a senior executive of a leading British fantasy role-playing game manufacturer. During our correspondence I had ample opportunity to observe and admire his obvious enthusiasm for children and his concern that they should not be harmed, least at all by the products over which he had control. His argument was that he was certain that the devil, in the sense of a personal, active force of evil in the world that could persuade human beings to do evil things, did not exist; and therefore—subject to basic considerations of decency and common sense—everything was legitimate material for play; if the occult was meaningless, horror was a pleasant distraction. It seems to me that this position, which is very common in the industry, brings much of the modern fantasy industry into conflict with biblical faith and indeed many other faiths.

5 'The Axeman: Your Letters', *G.M.* (July 1989), p. 81.

6 Charles Dickens, *A Christmas Carol* (1843).

7 Philip Carr-Gomm, *The Elements of the Druid Tradition* (Element, 1991), p. 39.

8 David Burnett, *Dawning of the Pagan Moon* (MARC/Monarch, 1991), p. 200. Many pagans are highly sceptical of the census figures.

9 Item on *Three Minutes*, ITV Meridian, transmitted 13 April 1993.

10 One of her novels, *The Beggar's Curse* (1984) is discussed in the present book—see p. 85.

11 *Ghostwatch*, BBC1 television, transmitted 31 October 1992.

12 Sue Arnold, 'Of Things that Go Bump in the Night' (*Radio Times*, 31 October–6 November 1992) p. 32.

13 John Parker, *At the Heart of Darkness: Witchcraft, Black Magic and Satanism Today* (Sidgwick and Jackson, 1993), p. 83.

14 *Daily Express* October 1986, *Sunday Mail* January 1988, *Daily Telegraph* March 1988, all quoted in Josh McDowell and Don Stewart, *Concise Guide to Today's Religions* (Scripture Press: rev. edn, 1988), p. 247.

15 From Summers' obituary in *The Times*, 11 August 1948.

16 Walton Hannah, *Darkness Visible* (Augustine Press, 1952): this book was the first of many in the general market that reprint Masonic secret rituals word-for-word. In making a comparison between public knowledge of witchcraft and public knowledge of Freemasonry I am not, of course, implying that they share common beliefs.

17 David Burnett, *Dawning of the Pagan Moon* (Monarch, 1991), p. 76.

18 *Ibid*, p. 87.

## Chapter 4

1 The obligation to hand out literature which one objects to yet has no right to withhold is one of the reasons why I eventually decided to leave Public Librarianship.

2 John Parker, *At the Heart of Darkness: Witchcraft, Black Magic and Satanism today* (Sigwick & Jackson, 1993). For those who feel they need to read further about LaVey's career and thought, Parker's book is a useful source. I have restricted myself to summarising aspects of his material which various other writers have also noted.

3 Many writers about the occult mention The Sorcerer's Apprentice, a highly influential occult retail outlet and world-wide mail-order business in Leeds which has over 40,000 clients, among them about 300 who describe themselves as satanists. It is run by a witch, Chris Bray. Its catalogue lists a very wide range of occult paraphernalia, books and accessories.

4 John Parker, *At the Heart of Darkness* (Sidgwick & Jackson, 1993), p. 315.

5 Andrew Boyd, *Blasphemous Rumours: is Satanic Ritual Abuse Fact or Fantasy? An Investigation* (Fount, 1992).

6 I have in mind accounts by social workers and carers whose allegations of child belief have been criticised because those making them are associated with a particular American view of satanic abuse; and also the accounts of writers such as Gabriele

Trinkle, whose *Delivered to Declare* (Hodder, 1986), was widely quoted in the early discussions of satanic abuse but was given little credibility by many professionals; she wrote as a committed Christian, claiming to have received supernatural release from a legacy of satanic childhood abuse.

7 This position was explained to me by an NSPCC spokesman.

8 'NSPCC and the Ritualistic Abuse of Children', NSPCC Press Release 17 July 1989.

9 Michael Baigent, Richard Leigh and Henry Lincoln, *The Holy Blood and the Holy Grail* (Cape, 1983).

10 This does not mean that the argument of the first half of the book is proven. Considerable doubt has been expressed about the quality of their research (misquotations, special pleading, abuse of sources, etc.), for example Philip Tait's very thorough review in *Evangelical Times* (May 1982). I am merely drawing attention to what appears to be two quite different mind-sets in the same book.

11 Story quoted in Paul de Parrie and Mary Pride, *Unholy Sacrifices of the New Age* (USA Crossway, 1988), p. 23; I have checked the story with Mrs Schaeffer. For a number of reasons I would take about ten percent of the book as substantial. It's a worrying ten percent.

## Chapter 6

1 Information taken from *Radio Times*, 31 October–6 November 1992.

2 Stephen King, *Night Shift* (New English Library, 1978), p. 17.

3 Joseph Grixti, *Terrors of Uncertainty: the Cultural Contexts of Horror Fiction* (Routledge, 1989), p. 26

4 For example Martin Barker, *A Haunt of Fears: the Strange History of the British Horror Comics Campaign* (Pluto Press, 1984).

5 Unfortunately I have no record of where this quote was made, though I noted its content at the time. I attempted unsuccessfully to obtain verification of the opinion from Mr Price.

6 Julian Fox, review of *Halloween* in *Films and Filming* (March 1979), p. 32.

7 Michael Mayo, review of *Hallowe'en Three* in *Cinefantastique* vol. 13 no 4 (April-May, 1983), p. 60.

8 M.R. James, ed. Gwendolen McBryde, *Letters to a Friend* (Arnold, 1956), p. 217.

9 Reprinted in the Lymington editions, for example *The Devil Rides Out* (1935: Hutchinson Lymington, 1963).

10 The references to Wheatley in John Parker's *At the Heart of Darkness* (Sidgwick and Jackson, 1993) provide examples of this.

11 Charles Williams, *All Hallows' Eve* (Faber & Faber, 1945).

12 *Ibid.*, p. 109.

13 Ann Pilling (writing as Ann Cheetham in early printings), *The Beggar's Curse* (Fontana Armada, 1984), p. 35.

14 *Ibid.*, p. 135.

15 *Ibid.*, p. 186.

## Chapter 7

1 Information given in a telephone conversation between the author and a Games Workshop staff member.

2 Iron Crown Enterprises, *Middle-Earth Role Playing* (ICE, 1985), sect. 1.1: 'What is a fantasy role playing game?'.

3 This is, for example, a problem with the material distributed by the American B.A.D.D. (Bothered about Dungeons and Dragons) organisation, who have sometimes mistaken a description of an occult activity for the thing itself. Similar reasoning would make most detective thrillers into handbooks on murder techniques.

4 Rupert Croft-Cooke, quoted in H.P. Lovecraft, *Omnibus 2: Dagon and other Macabre Tales* (Panther, 1985).

5 Jeff Grub, *Manual of the Planes* (TSR, 1987), p. 3.

6 I mean by this that there are certain books and individuals who are frequently cited by serious occult and arcane practitioners— for example, Aleister Crowley. A number of these references occur in fantasy role playing games, where they are being cited as credible sources.

7 Matthew Feigin, 'Dressing Up Your Arena for Hallowe'en', *Autuoduel Quarterly* (August 1991), p. 13.

8 Michael C. LaBossiere, 'Dark Hallowe'en', *Challenge: The Magazine of Science-Fiction Gaming* (3rd annual horror issue, October 1992), p. 32.

9 Lewis in particular has been criticised by some evangelical Christians and his work condemned as unbiblical and unreliable,

but these critics' arguments are invariably poor. A British author who takes this position is Roy Livesey, who in *More Understanding the New Age* (New Wine Press, 1990) uses a quotation from Lewis' Prince Caspian to argue that Lewis is opening doors to the occult: 'Men can go off the track' (p. 73). Livesey's case falls to pieces when one checks Lewis' original and finds that Livesey has omitted crucial words from his quotation—without indicating that he has left anything out.

10 J. Eric Holmes, *Fantasy Role Playing Games* (Arms and Armour Press, 1981), p. 99.

11 I have discussed the fantasy role-playing debate in some detail in *Children at Risk* (Kingsway, 2nd edn 1987), and some related issues in *Children at Play* (Kingsway, 1989).

12 Joe Williams and Kathleen Williams, *Lost Souls: Adventures in the Afterlife* (Marquee Press, 1991), back cover.

13 Jonathan Tweet and Mark Rein-Hagen, *Ars Magica* (Lion Rampant, 1989).

14 *Ibid.*, p. 5.

15 Christopher Early, *The Maleficium: the Sourcebook of the Infernal for Ars Magica 3rd Edition* (White Wolf, 1992), passim.

16 Jeffrey B. Russell, *A History of Witchcraft: Sorcerers, Heretics and Pagans* (Smith, 1983), p. 52.

## Chapter 8

1 Paul V. Beyerl, *A Wiccan Bardo: Initiation and Self-Transformation* (Prism, 1989), p. 3.

2 Philip Carr-Gomm, *The Elements of the Druid Tradition* (Element Books, 1991), p. 37.

3 The word 'snap' was suggested as the best translation by the commentator Arthur Jones in lecture notes produced in the 1970s.

## Chapter 9

1 A.A. Hoekema, *The Four Major Cults* (Paternoster Press, 1963), p. 1.

2 Irving Hexham and Myrtle Langley, 'Cracking the Moonie Code', *Credo*, September 1979.

3 Tim Cooper, *Green Christianity: Caring for the Whole Creation* (Hodder Spire, 1990), p. 117.

4 Nigel, Wiccan High Priest, contributor to *Hallowe'en: Trick or Treat* (Video, Jeremiah Films).

5 John Parker, *At the Heart of Darkness* (Sidgwick & Jackson, 1993).

6 Philip Carr-Gomm, *The Elements of the Druid Tradition* (Element Books, 1991), p. 82.

7 Alfred Watkins, *The Old Straight Track: its Mounds, Beacons, Moats, Sites and Mark Stones* (Methuen, 1925). This book is experiencing a revival in modern times, though it and several in the same vein have frequently been contradicted by modern archaeology which has identified supposedly ancient landmarks as being of relatively recent creation.

8 Douglas R. Hofstadter, *Godel, Escher, Bach: an Eternal Golden Braid* (Penguin, 1980).

9 Umberto Eco, *The Name of the Rose* (Secker & Warburg, 1983).

10 Stephen W. Hawking, *A Brief History of Time: from the Big Bang to Black Holes* (Bantam, 1988).

11 Jack Sparks (ed.), *The Apostolic Fathers* (Thomas Nelson, 1978), p. x.

12 Martin Reith (ed.) *God in Our Midst: Prayers and Devotions from the Celtic Tradition* (SPCK Triangle, 1975 reissued 1989), p. 9.

## Chapter 10

1 Taken from a contribution to *All Hallows' Eve*, documentary by BBC Radio Oxford, transmitted 29 October 1992. Used by permission of Mr Thomas.

2 Association of Christian Teachers, *Hallowe'en* (ACT, 1982), p. 4.

3 Margaret Cooling, *'Allo 'Allo, it's HALLOWE'EN again!* (ACT, 1988), p. 2.

4 From a telephone conversation with Mr Bryan, and incorporating material from *All Hallows' Eve* (n. 72 above). Used by permission. Mr Bryan would be willing to offer assistance to other churches planning similar events. He can be contacted through Christ Church, Northcourt Road, Abingdon, Oxfordshire.

5 Richard Morison, The CROPS Trust, 33 Harris Street, Peter-borough PE1 2LY. Mr Morison will make scripts, music and demonstration tapes available 'at a nominal cost', and interested readers should contact him direct.
6 Robert Farrar Capon, *The Supper of the Lamb* (Doubleday, 1969), p. 83.

# Dawning of the Pagan Moon

## by David Burnett

An investigation into the rise of Western paganism.

Paganism is a diffuse but growing movement in Britain and other parts of the Western world. David Burnett's careful assessment of this ancient religious tradition is scrupulously fair and balanced: 'I have listened to what people say and sought to understand what they have written,' he comments. 'The Neo-pagan movement can be likened to a fast flowing stream . . . it is an impossible task to draw up a neatly packaged description.'

In seeking understanding, Dr Burnett looks at the historical development of the pagan movement, modern pagan beliefs, the use of rituals and magic, the current pagan community in Britain, and relations between pagans and the Christian churches.

'My hope is that this book will act like a mirror,' writes David Burnett. 'To the pagan, I trust it will reflect his or her own position in both its strengths and its weaknesses.
'To the Christian, I hope the book will distinguish truth from stereotype. Many pagans criticise the Church as being unspiritual. What is the Christian response?'

Dr Burnett is a Fellow of the Royal Anthropological Institute, and lecturer at All Nations Christian College, Ware, Herts.

MARC
Monarch Publications

*Large format paperback*
£7.99
ISBN 1 85424 130 3

# Wrestling with Dark Angels

by C. Peter Wagner, F. Douglas Pennoyer, editors

Supernatural forces in spiritual warfare.

Christians are fighting in a cosmic war. It is far more real than our Western minds like to believe. In denying, or ignoring, the reality of the spirit world we have made ourselves vulnerable to the attacks of dark angels.

Until recently teaching on this issue from evangelical leaders has been skimpy or non-existent. In *Wrestling with Dark Angels* a number of respected theologians seek to redress the balance. They examine key aspects of spiritual warfare including power evangelism, territorial spirits, exorcism, sickness, deception and freedom in Christ.

'A superb and much-needed manual on spiritual warfare . . . a quite brilliant compilation.' Rev Kevin Logan, author of *Paganism and the Occult*

Monarch
Publications

*Large format paperback*
£8.99
ISBN 1 85424 128 1

# Warfare Prayer

## by C. Peter Wagner

Strategies for combating the rulers of darkness.

Since 1987 Dr Peter Wagner has been researching prayer. This is the first of four books resulting from that research, and deals with strategic-level spiritual warfare.

'Certain subjects are handled in some depth in this book which have so far not found their way into print,' he explains. 'I have included more *biblical material* here than I have found in any other book, partly because many are questioning whether there is biblical warrant for strategic-level spiritual warfare at all. The concepts of *spiritual territoriality* and the *naming of powers* have received considerable attention here. *Holiness* is frequently mentioned in other books, but rarely is it analyzed in the depth I believe is required for effective warfare prayer.'

Dr Wagner is Professor of Church Growth at Fuller Theological Seminary in California.

Monarch
Publications

*Large format paperback*
£7.99
ISBN 1 85424 173 7

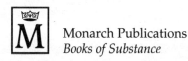

**Monarch Publications**
*Books of Substance*

All Monarch books can be purchased from your local general or Christian bookshop. In case of difficulty, they may be ordered from the publisher:

Monarch Publications
P O Box 163
Tunbridge Wells
Kent
TN3 0NZ

Please enclose a cheque payable to Monarch Publications for the cover price plus 60p for the first book ordered plus 40p per copy for each additional book ordered to a maximum charge of £3.00 to cover postage and packing (UK and Republic of Ireland only).

Overseas customers please order from:

Christian Marketing PTY Ltd
P O Box 154
Victoria 3215
Australia

Omega Distributors Ltd
69 Great South Road
Remuera
Auckland
New Zealand

Struik Christian Books
P O Box 193
Maitland 7405
Cape Town
South Africa

Kingsway USA Inc
4717 Hunter's Crossing Drive
Old Hickory
TN 37138
USA

Christian Marketing Canada
P O Box 7000
Niagara-on-the-Lake
Ontario L0S 1J0
Canada